EMERGING AGENDA FOR GLOBAL TRADE: HIGH STAKES FOR DEVELOPING COUNTRIES

T0303315

POLICY ESSAY NO. 20

EMERGING AGENDA FOR GLOBAL TRADE:

HIGH STAKES FOR DEVELOPING COUNTRIES

ROBERT Z. LAWRENCE, DANI RODRIK, AND
JOHN WHALLEY

DISTRIBUTED BY THE JOHNS HOPKINS UNIVERSITY PRESS
PUBLISHED BY THE OVERSEAS DEVELOPMENT COUNCIL
WASHINGTON, DC

Copyright © 1996 by Overseas Development Council, Washington, DC

Distributed by:
  The Johns Hopkins University Press
  2715 North Charles Street
  Baltimore, MD 21218-4319

Library of Congress Cataloging-In-Publication Data

Lawrence, Robert Z.
  Emerging Agenda for Global Trade: High Stakes for Developing Countries/ Robert Z. Lawrence, Dani Rodrik, and John Whalley

Policy Essay No. 20
Includes bibliographic references.

  1. International trade. 2. Competition—Government policy. 3. Labor policy. 4. Environmental policy—Economic aspects. 5. Foreign trade regulation. 6. Developing countries—Commerce. I. Rodrik, Dani. II. Whalley, John III. Title. IV. Series.

HF1379.L388   1996   382'.09172'4—dc20   96-41368

ISBN: 1-56517-014-8

Printed in the United States of America.

Director of Publications: Christine E. Contee
Publications Editor: Jacqueline Edlund-Braun
Edited by Jenepher Moseley
Cover design: Ripe Studios

Contents

Foreword

The successful completion of the Uruguay Round in 1993 represented the most extensive multilateral trade agreement in the history of commerce. After seven years of negotiation, GATT's 117 members reached consensus on many contentious issues, including for the first time, services, trade-related investment measures, and intellectual property. The Round had barely drawn to a close, however, when consideration began about the agenda of future multilateral negotiations.

Among the current highest profile issues the newly created WTO may choose to tackle are competition policy, labor standards, and trade and environment. ODC was fortunate to enlist three distinguished economists—Robert Z. Lawrence, Dani Rodrik, both of Harvard University, and John Whalley, of the University of Warwick—to consider the extent to which international rules in these new trade areas are needed, and the implications of for developing countries of the current and potential international provisions.

In *Emerging Agenda for Global Trade: High Stakes for Developing Countries*, Robert Lawrence argues that if an international agreement on competition policy was possible, developing countries would derive considerable benefits. Dani Rodrik examines the evidence and concludes that labor standards—or lack thereof—have consequences for trade and foreign investment patterns. He then considers whether a social-safeguards approach can be made to work for labor standards and suggests that the risks of not negotiating such a clause outweigh the dangers of an inappropriately designed process. Finally, John Whalley argues that the central issue for trade and the environment is whether developing countries should be compensated for policies encouraging environmental restraint.

ODC also wishes to acknowledge The Ford Foundation and The Rockefeller Foundation for support of the Council's overall program of which this essay is a part.

John W. Sewell
President
October 1996

Emerging Agenda for Global Trade

Emerging Agenda for Global Trade

Robert Z. Lawrence, Dani Rodrik, and John Whalley

This volume contains three studies by Robert Lawrence, Dani Rodrik, and John Whalley, all addressing the "new-new" issues on the emerging agenda for global trade negotiations that will eventually follow from the recently concluded Uruguay Round. The studies deal in turn with the three current highest profile issues: competition policy, labor standards, and trade and environment. In particular, they consider how developing countries could be affected.

The term "new-new" issues has come to refer to this grouping of issues, because the Uruguay Round itself dealt with its own set of new issues (services, trade-related investment measures, and intellectual property). Since the conclusion of the Round in late 1993, pressure has been building to place these "new-new" issues formally on the agenda of any future negotiations. And as the developing countries were cautious—and even fearful—of the Uruguay Round's new issues, discussing their interest in these new emerging issues at this juncture seems highly appropriate.

The studies emphasize how each of these issues represents a natural growth from the Uruguay Round process and decisions. The Round was precedent setting in linking trade policy, as a compliance mechanism, to nontrade objectives through the intellectual property decisions, and this continues with labor standards and trade and environment. Developing countries are fearful of these developments because trade barriers could increase against them, following determinations of violations of environmental and labor standard norms. They are concerned over measures that could truncate their growth and development to meet social policy objectives set in the developed world.

Before providing summaries of the individual papers, we focus in this introduction on the common factors that have placed these issues on the agenda and their implications for developing countries.

. . . .

DOMESTIC SOVEREIGNTY AND GLOBAL TRADE

■   THERE IS A PROFOUND TENSION in our world. It is organized politically into nation states, but increasingly the economy is global. This process of globalization has raised questions about how we should be governed. To what degree should policies be decided by nations independently and to what degree should they be subject to international agreement?[1]

TRADITIONAL APPROACH

The traditional answer to this question is to maximize the scope of national sovereignty and to focus international agreements on removing barriers to trade and investment. Today, indeed, border barriers for industrial products have almost disappeared among developed countries. Import quotas are rare and tariffs are low. Capital flows freely across the borders of most developed countries, and many developing countries and foreign investors are welcome in most. Throughout the developing world and former communist world, countries are embracing the international market. Although complete removal of border barriers has not yet been achieved, most nations agree in principle that free trade is desirable, and many are prepared to commit themselves to achieving it within the foreseeable future. In late 1994, for example, 34 nations in the Western Hemisphere and the 18 members of the Asia Pacific Economic Cooperation forum committed themselves to achieve full regional free trade and investment eventually.

When the barriers at nations' borders were high, governments and citizens could sharply differentiate international policies from domestic policies. International policies dealt with at-the-border barriers, but nations were sovereign over domestic policies without regard for effects on other nations. The General Agreement on Tariffs and Trade (GATT) emphasized this approach when it came to trade. Tariffs were to be reduced, but by and large, nations were left free to pursue domestic policies with regard to competition (antitrust), environment, and labor standards.

For developing countries, the GATT approach was attractive in principle, particularly once it was amended to provide for special and differential treatment. In principle, developing countries had considerable freedom to pursue whatever trade policies they chose. Although they are granted access to other countries at most favored tariff rates, developing countries can invoke special provisions to protect domestic industries in ways that would otherwise violate GATT rules. (In practice, however, the failure to make progress in liberalizing agriculture and measures such as the system of textile protection known as the Multifiber Arrangement, or MFA, actually discriminated against developing countries.)

Another feature of the traditional postwar approach was the principle that international trade policies should be treated separately from other issues. Although nations did conclude multilateral agreements on labor standards, business practices, and the environment, these agreements occurred outside the GATT, with compliance that was typically voluntary. This was the case, for example, when nations signed the conventions on labor standards in the International Labour Organization (ILO), the codes of conduct for multinational corporations at the United Nations, and, with a few noteworthy exceptions, in most international environmental agreements.

URUGUAY ROUND

The Uruguay Round multilateral trade negotiations, which ended in 1993, were the most extensive set of multilateral trade negotiations the world has seen. For developing countries the achievements in bringing agriculture under the disciplines of the trade rules and agreeing to eliminate MFA were particularly significant. Another noteworthy development was the agreement on intellectual property protection, which placed a new constraint on domestic sovereignty that could be enforced by the trading rules. Although developing countries were given more time to implement the new rules on intellectual property, in the long run, they were required to enforce the same measures as their more developed counterparts. The trade-related intellectual property rights (TRIPs) agreement was significant therefore, both because it established universal minimum standards for behind-the-border practices and because these are to be enforced by the international trade rules.

Even before the Uruguay Round agreement was completed, countries began to talk about new items for the negotiating agenda. Environment, labor standards, and competition policy all featured prominently. In 1991, the dormant working party of the GATT on trade and the environment originally set up in the early 1970s was reinvigorated and, at the meeting concluding the Uruguay Round in Marakesh in 1994, was charged with carrying out the work of the World Trade Organization (WTO) in this area. At the insistence of the United States and France, the issue of labor standards was introduced into the discussion at Marakesh, although no agreement was reached that the topic should be introduced to the agenda of the WTO through the establishment of a committee or working party. Nonetheless, calls continue to be heard for this to be done. Currently, at the Organisation for Economic Co-operation and Development (OECD), which has in the past been the location of preparatory discussions on trade policy, the Trade Committee has a program that includes work on competition policy.

DEEPER INTEGRATION

Why have these developments taken place? Developed countries have become increasingly linked not only through trade but also through foreign direct investment. Developing countries have universally shifted toward outwardly oriented policies, seeking to promote exports, reduce trade barriers, and encourage foreign investment. The result of this process of globalization has been pressure for deeper international economic integration. As international competition has intensified, firms, workers, and citizens have become increasingly aware that different national policies have international effects. When nations were separated by high border barriers and had little trade with each other, they could overlook what took place in each other's domestic affairs. As the barriers have come down, however, the impact of different domestic policies has become apparent. Increasingly, therefore, the call is for a "level playing field." The major political actors in society are business, labor, and environmental activists. When each of these groups sees different national rules affecting trade they are moved to cry foul. Pejorative terms are used to describe abhorrent foreign practices. For business, the problem is dumping; for labor, "social dumping"; and for environmentalists, "eco-dumping." All three groups are therefore seeking to achieve their goals, either by directly changing the trading rules, or by using trade as a weapon to enforce agreements achieved elsewhere.

In some cases, groups put forward these arguments as a pretext for protectionism. Their real goals are not an integrated international system based on rules, but a world economy that is fragmented on the pretext that national differences preclude fair competition. In other cases, however, there are more widely held social concerns about the impact of unfair competition, low labor standards, and lax environmental standards. One argument is that once markets and competition are global there is a strong case for the rules defining fair competition to be global. Similarly, as the world becomes increasingly aware of shared environmental problems such as global warming and the depletion of the ozone layer, the case for international coordination of environmental policies becomes stronger. Likewise, as labor markets become linked through immigration and trade and as international humanitarian concerns are raised because of improved publicity and communications—the CNN effect—the call for basic standards becomes stronger.

For developing countries the stakes in how these issues are handled in the international system are exceptionally high. Many in developing countries are understandably wary that adopting these measures could actually retard their development. A second concern is that these issues could become a pretext for protectionism that denies developing countries access to international markets. This could be the result unless sufficient recognition is made for the limited capacities with which many developing countries have to implement standards, regulations, and other policies in these areas. As a result of these concerns, a common response is to resist the introduction of the issues into the international trade agenda. It is common on issues of both environment and labor standards for representatives of developing countries to point out that when they were poor, the developed countries of today did not adhere to the norms they are trying to require of others. Similarly, there are others who feel that in a world dominated by developed-country multinationals, the adoption of tough competition rules could preclude government assistance for firms headquartered in developing countries.

There are, however, problems with these rejectionist responses because as countries without much international power, developing countries have an interest in seeing these issues decided in a multilateral setting with their participation. The absence of clear international rules could well provide opportunities for protectionists to influence their domestic policies. In addition, developing countries themselves have interests in a more competitive international market, a cleaner world, and labor standards that enhance welfare.

COMMON THEMES

It was for these reasons that we decided in this study to provide an introduction to these issues from the perspective of developing countries. Although the issues in this book each warrant the separate treatment they are given, several common themes are noteworthy.

DETAILS. In each of the areas we deal with in this book, it is difficult to come up with policy advice for developing countries absent the specific nature of the proposals of international agreement. The devil lies in the details. It is possible to conceive, in each area, agreements that could seriously reduce incomes in at least some developing countries: a competition rule policy that banned commodity cartels such as the Organization of Petroleum Exporting Countries (OPEC), an environmental rule that made developing-country products uncompetitive; or a global minimum wage set at a specific level that led to high unemployment. But there are also rules that would have positive or negligible effects that could facilitate trade by enhancing competition and limiting the use of these environment and labor standard arguments for protectionist purposes.

SCOPE. Another question each of these issues raises is what is the scope of the problem the rules should cover? As a general principle, the scope of governance should correspond to the scope of the policy problem so that all relevant considerations can be internalized. This emerges clearly in the environmental area. If the environmental problem is global, for example, the scope of policy should likewise be global. On other hand, the room for national diversity in treating purely local environmental issues is clearly greater. More problematic, however, are cases in which the international effects of labor standards or environmental practices are only felt indirectly. This might be through the impact on trade and investment flows of such standards and practices, or when behavior in one country offends the moral sensibilities of citizens in another.

RACE TO THE BOTTOM? Policy differences in each of these areas could well affect trade flows. Some fear the effect could be a race to the bottom in which competition drives standards to the lowest common denominator. There is a fear that competition could lead countries to relax standards as international competition grows. But in most cases, local diversity can be preserved as long as countries are willing to pay the cost. To be sure, the costs born by countries with higher standards will be higher, the stronger the international competition. Nonetheless, when it comes to the domestic environment, or degree of competition, or regulations for the labor market, under most likely international agreements, countries will remain free to impose standards that are higher than international norms.

TRADE SANCTIONS. Even where problems are global, the need to link their resolution to trade policies must be evaluated. Should trade sanctions be used to enforce adherence to environmental or labor standards, as their most enthusiastic proponents often argue, or would other mechanisms such as moral suasion, rewarding adherence, or adverse publicity and labeling be sufficient? In many examples, trade economists will point out that trade is often an imprecise method for dealing with the problem. For example, slave labor or deforestation may be problems, even when they do not affect trade flows directly. Taxing or banning such measures may be more effective than dealing with them through trade. On the other hand, proponents argue that trade sanctions may be the only international instrument that is available.

TRADE-OFFS. In each of these areas, it is often necessary to make tradeoffs between trade policy and other goals. On the one hand, proponents of other policies are concerned that trade policies sometimes have negative effects. The imposition of trade barriers such as quotas or other forms of managed trade such as voluntary export restraints sometimes reinforce domestic monopoly power. The GATT/WTO rules relating to standards, particularly when it comes to production processes, limit the ability of domestic authorities to restrict imports of products made in countries that do not have free trade unions, or that are made using processes (such as hormones for beef, or crops grown using toxic pesticides) that some believe to be dangerous. On the other hand, in each area, there are also concerns about links that affect trade because of particular aspects of domestic policy enforcement: for example, when domestic firms are granted waivers from antimonopoly rules and allowed to form cartels that restrict foreign entry, or when domestic labor or environmental standards have the effect of restricting or distorting trade.

CONSENSUS? These are very difficult issues, with many controversial aspects remaining unresolved. International agreement to deal with policies requires a consensus about the optimal direction policy should take. There are some limited areas in which such a consensus appears to exist. In the case of competition policies, examples are bans on price fixing and horizontal restraints; in labor standards, the ban on forced labor; and in environmental policies, the need for international cooperation on ozone depletion. But there are other areas in which considerable uncertainty remains: The need for labor standards relating to child labor, the appropriate competition policy vis-à-vis vertical restraints such as retail price maintenance, and the evidence on global warming and the correct response are all much more controversial issues.

THE BARGAIN. The nature of these new issues also poses new challenges for negotiation. They are different because unlike tariff reductions, they do not always fit neatly into the model of exchanges of concessions. In particular, it is straightforward to interpret the concept of special and differential treatment when it comes to tariff barriers, but when agreements involve rules, participants all eventually assume similar obligations. To be sure, less developed countries may be given more time to adjust, but eventually they will be expected to comply. Whereas trade liberalization generally makes both exporting and importing countries better off, when the rules are changed, some countries may lose while others gain.

This makes the overall package of rules to be negotiated of considerable importance. The Uruguay Round was a large package. Without concessions achieved on textiles and agriculture, for example, it would have been impossible to conclude an agreement on intellectual property. Not all rules are ideal for all parties. An important consideration therefore, is what is offered in return. If compensation is sufficient even rules that are damaging may be worth the price. In particular, whatever their interests on these issues, in return for major liberalization in agriculture and other issues of interest to developing countries, agreements might be attractive.

In sum, the complex nature of the issues raised in these essays makes generalizations difficult. They strike at the heart of the scope of national sovereignty. It is thus by no means clear that there will be international negotiations to establish rules that are tied to trade.[2] Some argue, in fact, there is no need for such deliberations since the GATT/WTO currently adequately covers each of these areas. In particular, failure to enforce competition policy could be dealt with under provisions for nullification and impairment of trade; and the standards code and Article XX already provide adequate coverage of environment.

However, because of the forces we have described above, there will continue to be pressures for international agreements. Moreover, in each policy area developing countries could benefit considerably from sensible international policies. International competition rules that enhance access to foreign markets, constrain restrictive business practices, and increase domestic competition at a time of deregulation and privatization could yield sizeable gains. International labor rules that stress fundamental human rights while recognizing the diversity of national circumstances and capabilities could contribute to global equity. Finally, international environmental agreements that provide developing countries with both incentives and the technological and financial assistance to comply could help achieve a cleaner world. Nonetheless, in each area there is also much that could go wrong. It therefore behooves developing countries to be vigilant in monitoring and participating in such negotiations since they have much at stake.

. . . .

SUMMARIES OF STUDIES ON COMPETITION, LABOR, AND ENVIRONMENT

■ THE SUMMARIES BELOW EXAMINE international provisions for competition policy, labor standards, and trade and environment, with particular reference to the ways in which developing countries could be affected.

COMPETITION POLICIES

In the first chapter, Robert Lawrence considers the arguments for an international agreement on competition policy and evaluates the implications for developing countries. Lawrence observes that eliminating trade barriers may be only a necessary and not a sufficient condition for ensuring that international markets are genuinely contestable. Removing border barriers may free foreign firms from the obligation to pay tariffs or the constraints of import quotas but foreign firms may find their ability to compete is impaired if domestic firms can fix prices, restrict output, allocate market shares, or engage in practices such as "tying" and "exclusive dealing" that prevent domestic distributors from carrying their products. Just as there is a case for international cooperation to achieve free trade, so too, there is a case for international cooperation in competition policies that aim at eliminating restrictive business practices.

Lawrence notes that the WTO currently does not require its members to meet binding obligations to implement competition policies. Indeed, most differ in their enforcement practices and many enforce none at all. The WTO does have rules on unfair pricing practices (i.e., antidumping) that are sometimes justified as a form of competition policy, but Lawrence argues that these are seriously deficient. In practice they often favor domestic firms and are actually detrimental to competition.

Lawrence notes that since competition is increasingly global, the decentralized application of competition policies through national bodies inevitably creates frictions. This inhibits the ability of firms to acquire and merge freely internationally because jurisdictions require different sets of information, use different standards (e.g., impact on domestic or international market concentration), and reach different conclusions. In addition, domestic competition laws typically focus on providing consumers with competitively priced products, but their ambit does not extend to consumers abroad. In most countries, in fact, domestic competition law often exempts collusion by domestic firms for sales abroad. Exporters can therefore fix prices and divide up international markets using practices that would be illegal at home. Countries also provide numerous exemptions to their domestic competition rules—a form of implicit subsidy that could enhance their competitiveness at the expense of foreigners. A single set of global rules would therefore provide more coherence than the current system.

Agreement on competition policies may be desirable—they are clearly on the post-Uruguay Round agenda—but it is still questionable whether an agreement is feasible. Lawrence observes that it has been possible to implement international agreements on competition policy within regional arrangements such as the European Union and the agreement between Australia and New Zealand. He also notes that international codes of corporate conduct have been agreed upon at the United Nations and the OECD. However, thus far, it has not been possible to implement a binding multilateral agreement. The problems and lacunae in the current system are clear, but the history of failure to reach agreement in this area suggest it will not be easy.

Nonetheless, Lawrence argues that if such an agreement was possible, developing countries could derive considerable benefits. In particular, developing countries would benefit, as exporters, if developed-country markets become more open, and as importers, if the restrictive practices of multinational corporations were restrained. In addition, international agreement could reinforce competition policy authorities at home. The case for such policies is strongest where markets are small and entry is difficult. This is particularly relevant for developing countries. Indeed, even absent an international agreement, developing countries are unilaterally moving to implement such policies and should be given the necessary technical assistance to do so.

LABOR STANDARDS

Most trade unionists and other labor representatives now accept that wage differences across countries based on labor-productivity differentials are legitimate and not cause for concern. The debate, therefore, has shifted to the area of labor market policies, and more specifically, labor standards.

It is alleged that exploitative practices in many low-wage exporting countries artificially depress labor costs, leading to unfair competitive advantage in world markets and a downward pressure on labor standards in rich countries. The practices most frequently cited include child labor, hazardous working conditions, absence of collective bargaining, and repression of labor unions. Trade economists respond to the clamor for labor standards by pointing out that there is very little economic rationale for the upward harmonization of labor standards. Countries with different sets of values and at different levels of income will naturally choose different labor market policies. Where there exists prima facie evidence of exploitative practices, most trade economists would argue that the appropriate manner in which to deal with such problems is through multilateral negotiations and that trade restrictions are likely to backfire by hurting precisely the groups they aim to protect. There are few areas of trade policy where the gap between the two sides of the argument is so wide and apparently so unbridgeable.

The chapter by Rodrik focuses on three questions. First, to what extent should labor standards in the South be a matter of concern for trade policy in the North? Second, is there any hard evidence that labor standards affect trade and investment flows? Third, what are the implications for policy, especially regarding unilateral versus multilateral approaches.

In thinking about these issues, Rodrik argues that it helps to demystify international trade by recognizing that from the perspective of any individual country the opening up of trade opportunities acts just like a technological advance. The goods that we sell abroad allow us to purchase imports in return, and hence our exports can be thought of as the inputs in a production function that are transformed into imports (the outputs). Prevailing international prices indicate the "input-output" coefficients used in this transformation. And, continuing the analogy, a terms-of-trade improvement (due, for example, to lower labor standards in a partner country) acts just like an advance in this technology, by reducing the input-output coefficients.

This perspective clarifies that the opening up of new trade opportunities is no different from the kind of technological progress that governments routinely pursue and encourage, even when such progress has sharp distributional considerations. At the same time, the analogy with technology clarifies a central issue: Nations do have collective preferences over what kinds of production technologies are admissible ("fair" or "legitimate"), and governments have always had restrictions on technologies that violate these boundaries, even on those that promise a large increase in a nation's productive potential. Since national laws and regulations always intrude on technology on grounds of fairness or legitimacy, it is difficult to see why a particular sort of technology, that which is embodied in international trade, should be considered immune from the same type of considerations. The implication is that weak labor standards in trade partners cannot be presumed to be of no consequence for domestic trade policy.

There is no universal, common definition of labor standards, but such standards are usually thought to cover areas like child labor, working conditions, and collective bargaining. The ILO Conventions come perhaps closest to representing a universal set of labor standards. Rodrik puts together a set of statistical indicators that relate to labor standards. Some of these are based on adherence to ILO Conventions, while the rest are taken from other databases and deal with either specific legislation or actual practices. He then uses these indicators to look for evidence that labor standards—or lack thereof—have consequences for trade and foreign investment patterns.

Rodrik presents three sets of results. First, there is some evidence that labor standards have statistically and economically significant effects on labor cost differentials across countries, even after controlling for labor productivity. Second, labor standards play a role in determining comparative advantage in labor-intensive products, with low-standard countries having a stronger revealed comparative advantage in such products, holding all else constant. Finally, labor standards have measurable consequences for flows of manufacturing foreign direct investment (FDI) as well, but the evidence here goes against the usual presumption: Low labor standards deter, rather than attract, FDI. In view of the weakness of the data on labor standards and the difficulties involved in quantifying differences across countries on such a complex set of issues, the results are overall quite suggestive.

Rodrik then turns to the question of whether a social-safeguards approach can be made to work in the area of labor standards. From the perspective of developing countries the main message of his chapter is: Do not worry about pressure on labor standards per se, but worry about protectionism that masquerades under the guise of a quest for improved labor standards. The former is not necessarily an indication of the latter and should not be confused with it. Once one is willing to believe that there is a valid distinction between these two, it becomes possible to design institutions that can respond to legitimate concerns in the North without undercutting the South's comparative advantage in labor-intensive products. In particular, Rodrik suggests that an appropriately designed social-safeguards clause is worth serious consideration. The key is to ensure that the process is transparent and open to those groups— exporters, consumers, and retailers—whose interests are aligned with an open trade regime. Provided broad representation can be achieved, a social-safeguards process at home can be a useful mechanism for eliciting social preferences over labor standards in trade partners. Developing countries should have little to fear from such a mechanism.

There is a risk in instituting a social-safeguards clause, but there is also a risk in not doing so. The latter risk is that increasing domestic pressures on labor (and environmental) matters will lead to a new set of "grey area" protectionist measures because there are no internationally agreed rules to channel these pressures into less harmful directions. If that happens, the consequences will be more damaging to developing-country interests than those of a social-safeguards clause negotiated multilaterally.

ENVIRONMENT

John Whalley traces out the recent surge in debate on the trade and environment link, highlighting the developing-country issues involved. Whalley identifies the recent focus on global environmental issues (global warming, deforestation, ozone depletion, biodiversity, oceans) as the force behind the drive by environmental groups in industrial countries to use trade measures to safeguard the environment.

The controversy over the trade and environment linkage revolves, first, around the extent to which expanded trade and environmental quality are inherently in conflict. On one hand, some in the environmental community contend that increased trade inevitably results in increased consumption and production and, hence, lowered environmental quality. On the other hand, the 1992 GATT annual report, for instance, argued that gains achieved through increased trade will increase real incomes; if these income gains are spent on environmental protection, higher rather than lower environmental quality may be the result.

A second aspect of the trade and environment debate is the extent to which trade policies are a valid mechanism through which to pursue improved resource management. Some argue that environmental problems are now so serious that their resolution is of paramount importance. The counter to this—usually advanced by trade policy practitioners—is that any special treatment for the environment introduced into existing trade rules sets a dangerous precedent. Fundamental to the debate is the question of "policy override," that is, whether some policy objectives are of such prime importance that they should dominate others.

The developing countries see the linkage of trade to environmental quality as driven largely by environmental interests in the higher income countries. Tension is growing between environmental advocates in industrial countries on the one hand, and, on the other, developing countries' with a strong interest in pursuing trade-led developmental strategies free from environmental restrictions. Developing countries emphasize that extensive economic liberalization has taken place in the developing world in the last decade and suggest that trade restrictions for environmental objectives run counter what they have been encouraged to do within the trading system.

Actions, such as the U.S. trade restrictions on tuna from Mexico and other countries with high incidental dolphin kills, have elevated the visibility of the trade issues in recent years, and Whalley foresees a growth in such future actions.

There are several implications for the trading system from the trade and environment linkage. First, there is a threatened fragmentation of the trading system from the introduction of nontrade issues into trade negotiation. Second, there is a need to clarify the application of existing trade rules to environmental issues. Finally, the evolving institutional linkages between the WTO, other global institutions, and emerging global treaties in the environmental arena have yet to be clarified.

Pressures may build for developing countries to enter a future negotiation in this area, and at the same time, provide the main target for such trade actions. Whalley emphasizes, however, that such a negotiation will be difficult to launch and for now remains ill focused in its specifics. Developing countries, therefore, will have time on their side to some degree in framing their response. The central issue, he suggests, is whether developing countries should be compensated for policies encouraging environmental restraint, or whether trade measures to coerce developing countries on environmental grounds are acceptable in the system. This he portrays as the issue of compensation or retaliation, suggesting its resolution rests on the extent to which property rights are determined to take precedence over the management of global environmental resources.

Notes

[1] For a more complete discussion of these issues, see Robert Z. Lawrence, Albert Bressand, and Takatoshi Ito, *A Vision for the World Economy: Openness, Diversity and Cohesion* (Washington DC: Brookings Institution, 1996).

[2] It is noteworthy that the U.S. government today is split on these questions. In particular, the U.S. Congress has resisted the efforts of the administration to explicitly introduce labor and environmental agreements into the negotiating authority given to the President to extend the NAFTA to Chile. In addition, the administration itself has been split on whether there should be multilateral agreements on competition policies. Although the Special Trade Representative has favored such an approach, the Justice Department prefers a bilateral approach.

Chapter 1

Competition Policies and the Developing Countries

Robert Z. Lawrence

With few exceptions, the efficient allocation of resources is fostered by competition.[1] By separating national markets, however, policies such as tariffs and quotas protect domestic firms and create incentives to charge higher prices and produce less output than under competitive conditions. Given the extent of the tariff and nontariff barriers that divided the world economy after the Second World War, therefore, it is no surprise that the focus of trade policies over the postwar period has been eliminating barriers at the border. But the elimination of trade barriers may be only a necessary and not a sufficient condition for ensuring that markets are genuinely contestable. What trade policy may grant, restrictive business practices may deny.

Free trade produces efficient results when markets are competitive. When there are monopolies, however, the benefits from trade are less clear. The removal of border barriers may free foreign firms from the obligation to pay tariffs or the constraints of import quotas. However, foreign firms may still find their ability to compete is impaired if domestic firms can fix prices, restrict output, allocate market shares, or engage in practices such as "tying" and "exclusive dealing" that prevent domestic distributors from carrying their products. What free trade may grant to importers, domestic cartel arrangements and other restrictive practices may deny.

. . . .

COMPETITION POLICIES

■   COMPETITION (OR ANTITRUST) POLICIES aim at eliminating such restrictive business practices. Specifically such policies try to prevent agreements between firms that limit competition or the abuse of dominant position by individual firms.[2] The failure to enforce such policies by domestic authorities is thus a matter of concern for those seeking free trade.

Just as there is a case for international cooperation to achieve free trade, so too, there is a case for international cooperation in competition policies. In fact, the original trade rules for the postwar era, the Havana Charter establishing a new International Trade Organization (ITO), contained a section that dealt with restrictive business practices.[3] These rules were seen as particularly necessary given the widespread existence of cartels in the 1930s. However, the Havana Charter was never adopted and the GATT, which dealt only with international practices such as dumping and subsidies, constituted the basic rules of the postwar trading system.

Competition policies were also seen as an essential ingredient for creating the European Common Market. EC Treaty competition rules were therefore implemented to prevent private firms from establishing substitutes for the trade barriers that the treaty removed, and the Treaty of Rome, signed in 1958, placed authority for the conduct of trade-related competition policies under the jurisdiction of the European Commission.

International agreements on competition policy have been negotiated bilaterally and regionally with varying degrees of commitment. The United States has signed several bilateral agreements with other nations calling for communication on, and coordination of, competition policy enforcement—most notably a cooperation agreement signed with the European Union (EU) in 1991.[4] In the bilateral negotiations between the United States and Japan known as the Structural Impediments Initiative, the United States demanded and obtained a Japanese commitment to increase the power and enforcement activities of Japan's Fair Trade Commission.

At the regional level, formal arrangements have been negotiated most notably within the EU, between the EU and the nations of Scandinavia (in the 1994 Agreement for a European Economic Area), and between the EU and Eastern European nations. The 1983 Closer Economic Relations (CER) Agreement between Australia and New Zealand substituted cooperation in antitrust for the elimination of antidumping and countervailing duties.

At the multilateral level, however, progress toward common competition rules has been slow. In 1953, a committee comprising delegates from six industrialized nations (including the United States) plus four developing countries (India, Mexico, Pakistan, and Uruguay) produced a U.N. draft convention.[5] However, it was never ratified by the United States because of opposition from the business community. Several subsequent multilateral efforts have also failed, most notably an effort at the GATT in 1960.[6] In 1980, the United Nations General Assembly adopted, after many years of negotiation, a nonbinding set of multilaterally agreed equitable principles and rules for the control of restrictive business practices.[7]

In the Uruguay Round, several agreements contain recognition of the potentially important role played by competition policies, but they impose no binding commitments on members. For example, the General Agreement on Trade in Services (GATS) recognizes that business practices of service suppliers may restrain competition and thus trade in services but requires members, on request, only to enter into consultations and to provide publicly available information.[8] A key issue for the future is whether the post-Uruguay Round negotiating agenda of the WTO should aim at achieving an agreement on competition policy.

REASONS FOR AN INTERNATIONAL AGREEMENT ON COMPETITION POLICY

There are several reasons why such an agreement might be desirable. The WTO currently does not require its members to meet binding obligations to implement competition policies. Indeed, most differ in their enforcement practices and many enforce none at all. While the GATT/WTO does not contain explicit agreements on competition policy, it does have rules on antidumping and trade distorting subsidies. These antidumping rules are sometimes justified as a form of competition policy governing predatory prices, but in practice they often favor domestic firms and are actually detrimental to competition. One strong reason for adopting an international agreement on competition policies would be, at the same time, to eliminate the antidumping rules. Although in practice this will not be easy, since domestic firms who benefit from the anti-dumping rules are bound to resist.

Under these rules, dumping is defined either as selling exports at prices below those charged at home (i.e., price discrimination) or selling at below cost in a manner that causes material injury to domestic firms with which it competes. The remedy for dumping is the levying of an offsetting tariff.

There are some difficulties, however, in understanding the ratio-nale for these rules. One problem is that the ability to price discriminate suggests that the exporter actually has market power *at home*. But the antidumping rules respond not by lowering prices in the home market but by raising them in the foreign market. A competition policy focus would try to reduce that power by requiring the exporter's government to take action. A second problem is that under the antidumping rules, predation is never explicitly investigated and one of the tests it applies, selling below costs, is not an adequate indication of predatory intent. Indeed, the cost definition applied is often that of average costs, but economic theory suggests that under competitive conditions, in the short run, competitive firms will have prices that equal marginal costs and that could fall below average costs. Thus firms may be found guilty of dumping while simply acting in a manner typical of competitive markets. Moreover these same rules do not apply to domestic firms. Consequently, domestic firms are able to sell at prices for which foreign firms with exactly the same costs and prices will be sanctioned. In addition, the antidumping rules reflect the concerns of producers who compete with imports rather than those of consumers. They deal with problems that arise when exported goods are priced too low, but not when they are sold at too high a price.

Relying on domestic competition policies alone, however, would also leave some important gaps. First, although unlike antidumping laws, domestic competition laws do focus on providing consumers with competitively priced products, their ambit does not extend to consumers abroad. In most countries, in fact, domestic competition law actually exempts collusion by domestic firms for sales abroad.[9] Exporters can therefore fix prices and divide up international markets using practices that would be illegal at home. Indeed, under some circumstances, governments may actually compel their exporters to adhere to voluntary import restraints (VRAs) and importing authorities may exempt such arrangements from their competition rules.[10] For example, foreign firms selling in the United States that participate in cartels and VRAs under instructions from their home government can claim "sovereign compulsion" and thus receive immunity from U.S. antitrust rules. Finally, countries also provide numerous exemptions to their domestic competition rules—a form of implicit subsidy that could enhance their competitiveness at the expense of foreigners. In most developed countries these exemptions apply to research and development ventures, and in Japan exemptions are granted to industries in recession and those needing rationalization.

Since competition is increasingly global, the decentralized application of competition policies through national bodies inevitably creates frictions. Many mergers and acquisitions involve firms from more than one country.[11] Firms may therefore have to obtain permission in several jurisdictions before undertaking such mergers. This inhibits their ability to acquire and merge freely because jurisdictions require different sets of information, use different standards (e.g., impact on domestic or international market concentration), and reach different conclusions.

Some countries, most notably the United States, have tried to deal unilaterally with the absence of an international agreement in this area through extraterritorial means, giving rise to jurisdictional conflicts with other countries. In 1992, the Department of Justice published new guidelines indicating that it would challenge foreign businesses that engaged in practices that harmed U.S. exports—if such practices would have violated U.S. antitrust laws had they occurred in the United States.[12] In the past, these U.S. efforts have been met by foreign actions that have sought to block the application of U.S. laws to their domestic industries.

Finally, there is no entity currently responsible for ensuring that global markets are competitive. Thus if the world market for a product were to be monopolized or cartelized, and if no single national government desired or was able to take action, such practices would escape sanction. Indeed, the absence of such an authority has led individual nations to try to ensure against vulnerability to such practices through industrial policies. Examples include the development of Sematech by the United States partly in response to perceived dominance by Japan of semiconductor equipment manufacturing, and the sponsorship of Airbus by the EU in response to U.S. dominance in aircraft.

A single set of global rules could, in principle, provide more coherence than the current system. If effective rules could be negotiated, they would improve market access for foreign firms, present an opportunity for the elimination of antidumping rules, and allow countries to avoid second-best measures of industrial policy. In sum, therefore, in this view, an international agreement on competition policies is called for. Such an agreement would be particularly attractive if as in the case of the EU and the CER agreement between Australia and New Zealand, it would be possible at the same time, to eliminate the application of antidumping and countervailing duty rules.

REASONS AGAINST AN INTERNATIONAL AGREEMENT ON COMPETITION POLICY

Competition policies have been attacked both by those who believe in free markets and those who do not. On the one hand, such policies are often seen as unnecessary by many from the free market school. Those holding such views argue that most markets are actually contestable and the cases in which cartels or cartel-like arrangements can be effective are few and, even then, likely to be temporary. Moreover, those advancing such views are concerned by the danger that government policies may be captured by firms and may actually serve to reinforce rather than reduce monopoly power. In this view, the exceptions granted by competition policy authorities could actually become the rule and serve to entrench monopolies rather than remove them. In addition, particularly in the area of vertical restraints, practices once viewed as objectionable may actually be justified as efficient. There is also a fear that an international agreement would enshrine the lowest common denominator rather than a strong policy.

On the other hand, those skeptical of free markets will also oppose such an agreement for the very reasons that liberals seeking freer markets would support it. In particular, the application of competition policies would make trade protection (and other industrial policies) more difficult. It is sometimes pointed out that while the goal of competition policies is to promote competition, the goal of trade policies is usually to promote competitors. One set of objections, therefore, comes from those seeking to protect the special interests who are hurt by international trade. As border trade barriers have been reduced, invoking the antidumping laws has become the protectionist trade instrument of choice. Similarly, in almost all countries, competition rules outlaw market sharing arrangements. And yet, when they impose voluntary export restraints (VERs), national governments of the same countries are actually implementing precisely such an agreement.

A second set of objections comes from those who believe in a stronger role for government policies to compensate for market failures. An international agreement could grant antitrust exemptions for policies designed to correct such failures, but proponents of intervention might fear such agreements could be unduly constraining.

A different set of objections stems from those who believe that the administration of competition laws should not or cannot be centralized. Some of these views are expressed by domestic antitrust practitioners.[13] There is a view common among many lawyers that national competition policies and administrative procedures are simply too diverse to permit the degree of harmonization required for international agreement. Reflecting the consensus in economic theory about their effects, national rules are quite similar on issues relating horizontal restraints such as price fixing and cartels. (In the United States, the European Union, and Japan, price fixing and market sharing are illegal and predation is prohibited.) But, partly because of the greater theoretical uncertainty, the treatment of vertical restraints, such as retail price maintenance, exclusive dealing, and territorial restraints, is much more varied. Indeed, in many countries these rules are implemented on a case-by-case basis rather than per se.[14] In addition, rules for dealing with mergers and defining dominant positions differ as does the means for implementing policies—with the United States relying heavily on judicial action while the EU and Japan place more emphasis on administrative actions.[15] Moreover, some argue that such diversity is appropriate, given different national historical traditions and circumstances.[16]

A related view reflects concerns about national sovereignty. There are many who are reluctant to assign increased authority to an international body at the expense of national authorities. In particular, some stress the role played in the European Union by the willingness of the national European governments to accept the disciplines imposed by Brussels.[17] It is doubtful whether the broad range of nations represented in the WTO would be similarly willing to accept such disciplines. Moreover, particularly if competition rules were to replace antidumping and countervailing duties rules, governments would have to reach agreements on the application of subsidies that go much further than those achieved in the GATT/WTO.

Alexis Jacquemin argues that the extreme diversity of opinion on national industrial policies reduces the probability of establishing minimum standards and enforcement of competition policies.[18] He notes that in almost all nations, governments implement industrial policies through subsidies, public procurement, programs for cooperative research and development, and support for small and medium enterprises, and the use of defenses for mergers such as "in the public interest" or "improving efficiency." The key issue for many countries, therefore, is the degree to which commitments to implement competition policies would constrain such activities.

Finally, there is the argument that the GATT (and the new WTO) involve systems based essentially on an international agreement that, with the exception of disputes adjudication, is independently administered by national governments. For a genuinely global competition policy, concerned with controlling international cartels and monopolies, nations would either have to act together or an independent authority would probably be required. Such a policy would require considerably more power and competence than the WTO currently posses.

OPTIONS

These arguments suggest that despite its merits, achieving a comprehensive global competition policy might not be feasible. Nonetheless, progress could be made internationally even in the absence of a comprehensive competition policy code that was enforced multilaterally. First, there is scope to improve cooperation and centralize data collection between national competition policy authorities. Second, there could be agreements providing for international oversight of implementing policy on domestic competition rather than international rules. In the NAFTA, for example, trinational panels serve as appeal boards for domestic applications of antidumping and countervailing duty rules and domestic enforcement of labor and environmental standards. Similarly in cases involving international firms, countries might agree to allow appeals to an international body to adjudicate the application of domestic rules. Third, there is the opportunity to undertake increased cooperation through bilateral and regional agreements when there may be smaller differences in antitrust laws and a greater willingness to limit national sovereignty. Fourth, members of the WTO could simply agree not to use domestic law to enforce international cartel agreements (i.e., to deny sovereign compulsion as a defense). This would be a minimal approach to the cartel issue.[19] The American Bar Association has recommended instead that countries repeal laws granting immunity to export cartels and prosecute cartel conduct, both at home and for export markets. Fifth, an international agreement could be limited to the issues of price discrimination and predation, which would allow the elimination of current antidumping rules. In all these cases, international measures would only be taken in large cases with international implications. In many markets, competition is a purely local concern, and there is no reason why an international body should get involved.

Sixth, an agreement could be negotiated multilaterally that would lay out a set of minimum standards for national policies that reflected areas in which an international consensus exists. Individual nations could then be given leeway to apply more stringent policies in areas of agreement and independent policies in areas where no such agreement is possible. In addition, in these latter areas, agreements on international oversight could be provided.

Finally, F. M. Scherer has suggested a more ambitious approach.[20] He proposes creation of an international competition policy office (ICPO) that would initially gather information and later investigate anticompetitive behavior. (Although he does not propose it, Scherer's ICPO could also be given the power to impose sanctions.) Scherer emphasizes the importance of proceeding simultaneously with both cartel and merger policies. All cartels and companies with large shares of world export markets would register with the ICPO. Later all companies planning to merge would also have to register. Nations that think trade has been restrained would petition the ICPO for redress. Initially, the ICPO would cooperate with local authorities and recommend actions. Later, it would be given power to intervene in cases with serious implications for global markets.

The ICPO would encourage domestic authorities to deal with most cases independently. It might, however, form international panels to arbitrate cases where parties claimed that others had violated internationally agreed norms or that domestic laws had not been adequately enforced.

Nonetheless, although these policies would provide considerable benefits to U.S. firms, American multinational firms concerned about market access would not find them a panacea. Elimination of the antidumping rules would aid the many U.S. exporters who are now subject to foreign antidumping actions, while removing hidden protection for importers. However, the difficulties of obtaining international agreement on vertical restraints would probably limit the benefits from improved access. In addition, even in the United States, as noted by the Council of Economic Advisors, "competition" and not entry opportunities for individual firms is protected under U.S. antitrust law.[21] In the absence of evidence of restraints on competition in the domestic market, it may be difficult to win a case on the grounds that a new firm cannot gain entry. In addition to a multilateral competition policy initiative, therefore, it may be necessary to pursue these access issues bilaterally, particularly with

countries such as Japan, in which restraints appear to represent significant obstacles to access.

. . . .

IMPLICATIONS FOR DEVELOPING COUNTRIES

■   THIS POLICY DISCUSSION raises two important questions for
developing countries. First, what would such international agreements on
competition policy mean for developing countries as participants in international markets? Second, what would it mean for their domestic economic policies? Let us consider these in turn.

INTERNATIONAL MARKETS

The central goal in implementing competition policies internationally is to make world markets more contestable. As relative newcom-
ers to many markets, developing countries have a distinct interest in seeing this goal accomplished. Controls on the power of dominant firms and
groups of firms are generally beneficial for those with whom they compete. From this viewpoint, therefore, more open developed-country markets would yield benefits to developing-country exporters. The greatest
benefits for developing countries as exporters would come if competition
law was to replace the application of antidumping rules, which have
become increasingly important constraints on developing-country
exports.

Developing countries would also gain as importers. Since they
generally have smaller markets, developing countries may offer tempting
opportunities for firms with market power to allocate territories. Indeed,
many developing countries may be too small to support the fixed costs
of entry by several firms and therefore be particularly vulnerable to
monopoly suppliers in the first place. In addition to such cost-based barriers, however, freed from oversight by their national authorities, firms
from developed countries could also collude to split up markets and
refrain from competing. In response to concerns expressed by developing
countries in the 1960s and 1970s about the anticompetitive practices of

multinationals (through restricting technology transfer and monopoly pricing) voluntary codes of conduct for multinational corporations were issued by the United Nations and the OECD. An international competition policy with teeth would be a far more effective means of addressing these issues.

On the other hand, developing countries have themselves participated in international cartels—the most famous of which is the Organization of Petroleum Exporting Countries (OPEC). The application of antitrust to such cartels in which they participate would presumably damage such producers by reducing their ability to cartelize. Trade in services such as maritime shipping and air transportation are also governed by cartel arrangements in which developing countries participate. However, neither OPEC nor other commodity price arrangements have been particularly effective over the long run, and in any case, undoubtedly, some type of exemption could be sought.

DOMESTIC MARKETS

The second set of advantages of an agreement would come from its impact on the domestic markets of developing countries. There is a growing awareness in many developing countries that increased attention to competition policy is called for. Because the need for such policies is probably greater than in many developed countries, developing countries would derive considerable benefits from adhering to the disciplines that such an international agreement might require.

Scale is an important determinant of competition. In sectors where scale economies are important, the size of the market determines the number of firms that can be supported. Since they can support fewer firms, small markets will be more concentrated and thus less competitive than large markets. These considerations point to the need for both free trade and competition policies in developing countries. Smaller countries are more constrained by the size of their domestic markets. The gains from entering trade are generally proportionately larger for small countries than for large. By opening themselves to competition internationally, developing countries take major steps in making their domestic markets for tradable goods more contestable. By opening themselves to international investment they may also increase competition in their non-traded sectors.

Competition in domestic markets for non-traded goods is often particularly lacking because of domestic collusion, distribution monopolies, and other vertical restraints.[22]

Competition policies can play an important role in keeping domestic distribution systems from acting like private tariff-collection agencies and restraining trade through such practices as preventing parallel imports and applying high markups to imported products. Of course, all these benefits from competition policies depend on the ability of the enforcement authorities to resist efforts by firms to capture the process, obtain exemptions, and thus inhibit rather than increase competition.

There is a growing recognition throughout the developing world of the importance of competition policies. These policies are increasingly being implemented in Asia, Eastern Europe, and Latin America.[23] Although in many countries implementation problems arise because of scarcities in resources and enforcement experience.[24] A large number of countries have been using UNCTAD assistance in implementing these policies.[25] Countries could of course simply implement such policies unilaterally, but the existence of an international agreement to which nations could subscribe would bring several advantages. First, if the agreement conferred advantages such as relief from foreign antidumping and countervailing duties, it would provide an incentive to adopt such rules. Second, the agreement would set an international standard that could guide countries in determining which policies should be implemented. Third, an agreement would make domestic policies more credible and permanent. Countries may adopt policies but an international agreement can prevent backsliding. Finally, by setting a common standard, an agreement would make policies more similar internationally, thereby facilitating coordination and eventual harmonization.

OBJECTIONS

Since many developing-country markets are highly concentrated and lack adequate competitive pressures, there will undoubtedly be many firms who will object on self-serving grounds to the adoption of more binding competition policies. It would not be surprising, therefore, if many developing countries oppose such an agreement, despite the benefits alluded to above. However, there also may be more legitimate grounds for concern.

In many developing countries (as in many developed countries) governments routinely apply industrial policies that are generally justified on the grounds of market failures. These include policies to promote national champion firms, preferential government procurement, subsidies, preferential tax treatments, licensing of permits for domestic investment, foreign exchange, import quotas, etc. In nations such as Korea (and earlier Japan), access to a high-priced domestic market has been used as an indirect method of subsidizing favored domestic firms.[26] Adherence to a meaningful set of obligations for international competition policy would inevitably constrain such policies. Developing countries would therefore be faced with a choice of accepting such constraints to obtain the benefits of participating in an international competition policy regime, or of remaining outside it.

This tradeoff will appear different in different countries. In those where industrial policies appear to have failed, adopting such a constraint would be beneficial. In others, where more success has been achieved, the costs would be higher. It is likely and desirable that countries will make different choices, depending on their circumstances.

Unlike traditional GATT agreements on lowering tariffs, negotiations for establishing new regimes for rules do not fit neatly into a system involving a mutual exchange of concessions or a system that provides developing countries with special and differential treatment. It is also possible, that if such an agreement is adopted, not all members of the WTO will receive unconditional most favored nation treatment. Indeed, if an agreement eliminates the antidumping and subsidies rules in return for adherence to competition policy rules, the exports of those nations not participating in such an agreement would undoubtedly remain subject to the antidumping provisions. (This can be inferred from the fact that antidumping rules continue to prevail in the NAFTA and in the agreements between the European Union and Eastern European nations.) This would create a two-tier international system with one group of countries more deeply integrated than the other. [27]

An alternative and more desirable outcome from the standpoint of the developing countries would be for the developed countries to eliminate their antidumping and countervailing duties for developing countries (or at least, for the least developed countries), giving the developing countries a generous period of time in which to meet competition policy disciplines or tying adherence to the competition policy disciplines to a particular level of development. The former solution would sustain the major accomplishment of the Uruguay Round in placing all contracting parties under similar disciplines and follow the precedent set in the agreement on intellectual property (TRIPs).

. . . .
CONCLUDING COMMENTS

■ ALTHOUGH COMPETITION POLICIES are clearly on the post-Uruguay Round agenda, it is still questionable whether an agreement is feasible. The problems and lacunae in the current system are clear, but the history of failures to reach agreements in this area suggest it will not be easy. It is noteworthy that when a multinational group of experts recently came up with a draft proposal they received considerable criticism from many quarters.[28] There are not only conceptual obstacles to framing an agreement; the political obstacles to achieving it remain considerable. Most major initiatives to change the trade rules over the postwar period have been led by the United States. It is also noteworthy, therefore, that the U.S. Department of Justice has been particularly unenthusiastic about a multilateral agreement in this area. The delegation of ultimate authority over competition policy to an international body or agreement is not a step that nations will or should take lightly. Although competition may have become global, the world remains divided into nations that do not easily yield sovereignty.

Nonetheless, if such an agreement was possible, developing countries could derive considerable benefits. The case for such policies is strongest where markets are small and entry is difficult. Indeed, even absent an international agreement, developing countries are unilaterally moving to implement such policies and should be given the necessary technical assistance to do so.

Notes

I am grateful for comments received on an earlier draft from Carlos Primo Braga, Catherine Gwin, Raymond Vernon, Sidney Weintraub, and John Whalley.

[1] As is well recognized, markets may not perform efficiently when there are externalities, public goods, and monopolies.

[2] Horizontal restraints are monopolistic practices such as fixing prices, allocating markets, rigging bids, and abuse of a dominant position; vertical restraints involve practices between suppliers and distributors such as retail price maintenance an exclusive territory arrangements.

[3] The agreement allowed members to present complaints relating to various forms of horizontal restraints on trade such as fixing prices or terms of sale, excluding firms, dividing territories, limiting production, preventing (by agreement) the development or application of technology, and discriminating against particular enterprises. The ITO was also to carry out studies relating to the impact of restrictive practices on trade.

[4] F. M. Scherer, "Integrating National Economies: Promises and Pitfalls," in *Competition Policies for an Integrated World Economy* (Washington, DC: The Brookings Institution, 1994), p. 40.

[5] Ibid., p. 39.

[6] Experts at GATT investigated the possibility of agreements on Restrictive Business Practices but rejected these because of the absence of a necessary consensus and the fact that countries did not yet have sufficient experience of action in this field to devise an effective control procedure. See John H. Jackson, William J. Davey, and Alan O. Sykes, *Legal Problems of International Economic Relations: Cases, Materials, and Text* (St. Paul, MN: West Publishing, 1995), p. 1093.

[7] See UNCTAD document TD/RBP/Conf 10/Rev1 (New York: United Nations, 1981).

[8] See Bernard Hoekman and Michel M. Kostecki, "The Political Economy of the World Trading System: From GATT to WTO," mimeo, 1995.

For a more complete analysis of the links between competition policy and the Uruguay Round agreements, see UNCTAD, "The Outcome of the Uruguay Round: An Initial Assessment," *Supporting Papers to the Trade and Development Report 1994* (New York: United Nations, 1994), pp. 240–42.

[9] In the United States, the Webb-Pomerene Act (covering collective export sales) and Export Trading Company Act allow conduct that would otherwise violate U.S. law. The same is true under Article 85 of the Treaty of Rome, which exempts export cartels that do not affect trade between member states or the common market.

[10] Compare the restrictions in the U.S. Sherman Act, which flatly prohibit price fixing or agreements and market sharing arrangements, with the Voluntary Restraint Arrangement for automobiles, for example, in which the Japanese government was required to set quotas (i.e., market shares) for each of the Japanese automakers.

[11] According to Scherer, op. cit., p. 2, the Gillette Company's acquisition of Wilkinson Sword had to be cleared by 14 distinct merger offices.

[12] Previously U.S. policy had been understood to prevent challenges to anticompetitive practices in foreign markets unless there was direct harm to U.S. consumers. Arvind Subramanian, "The International Dimension of Competition Policies," *International Organization*, Vol. 49 (Spring 1995), pp. 315–51.

[13] In 1991, a special committee on international antitrust of the American Bar Association concluded no initiative on a world code should be pursued.

[14] See Diane P. Wood, "International Competition Policy in a Diverse World: Can One Size Fit All?" in Jackson, Davey, and Sykes, op. cit.

[15] Graham and Richardson argue that the clearest economic cases can be made for issues relating to cartelization, mergers, and acquisitions. They believe convergence on monopoly, other horizontal restraints, and price fixing rules are also possible. They are more skeptical about the opportunities in the area of vertical restraints. Edward M. Graham and J. David Richardson, "Summary of Project on International Competition Policy," paper submitted to Joint Roundtable of the Committee on Competition Law and Policy and the Trade Committee, OECD, Paris.

[16] Wood, op. cit.

[17] Kalypso Nicolaidis and Raymond Vernon, "Competition Policy and Trade Policy in the European Union," Harvard University Faculty Papers R95-9 (Cambridge, MA: Kennedy School of Government, July 1994).

[18] Alexis Jacquemin, "Comments on Scherer," in *Competition Policies for an Integrated World Economy*, op. cit., pp. 99–110.

[19] Scherer, op. cit.

[20] Ibid.

[21] *Economic Report of the President* (Washington, DC: U.S. Government Printing Office, February 1995), p. 246.

[22] Gausch and Rajapatirana give an example from Colombia of Nabisco being forced to distribute through Colombian food distributors and thus domestic producers capture trade benefits as rents. See J. Luis Gausch and Sarath Rajapatirana, *The Interface of Trade, Investment, and Competition Policies: Issues and Challenges for Latin America*, Policy Research Working Paper No. 1393 (Washington, DC: World Bank, 1994), p. 10.

[23] For Asia, see Edward N. Graham, "Competition Policies in the Dynamic Industrializing Economies: The Cases of China, Korea, and Chinese Taipei," paper prepared for OECD Development Centre, Paris, 1995.

In Eastern Europe, Bulgaria, Czech Republic, Hungary, Poland, Rumania, and Slovak Republic have negotiated association agreements with the EU that require these countries to adopt the basic competition rules of the EU for practices affecting trade between them and the EU. As noted by Hoekman and Mavroidis, these relate to agreements between firms restricting competition, abuse of dominant position, behavior of state-owned firms and competition-distorting state aids (Articles 85, 86, 90, and 92 of the EEC Treaty). Almost all these countries have passed laws and assigned responsibility for their enforcement. In addition, Lithuania and the Russian Federation have implemented such policies. See Bernard Hoekman and Petro C. Mavoidis, "Linking Competition and Trade Policies in Central and East European Countries," Discussion Paper No. 1009 (United Kingdom: Centre for Economic Policy Research, 1994).

Other such countries include Argentina, Brazil, Chile, Colombia, Fiji, Gabon, India, Ivory Coast, Jamaica, Kenya, Mexico, Pakistan, Peru, Republic of Korea, Sri Lanka, Thailand, Tunisia, Venezuela (see UNCTAD, op. cit.). For a description of policy developments in several developing countries, see Susan K. Sell, "Intellectual Property and Antitrust in the Developing World," *International Organization*, Vol. 49 (Spring 1995), pp. 315–51.

[24] Gausch and Rajapatirana, op. cit.

[25] Sell 1995.

[26] For a debate on these policies, see Albert Fishlow, Catherine Gwin, Stephan Haggard, Dani Rodrik, and Robert Wade, *Miracle or Design? Lessons from the East Asian Experience*, Policy Essay No. 11 (Washington, DC: Overseas Development Council, 1994).

[27] One possibility, therefore, would be to reach such an agreement in a setting different from the WTO, perhaps in the OECD, and to grant a special waiver from the MFN requirement in the WTO for members participating in the competition policy arrangement.

[28] See Jackson, Davey, and Sykes, op. cit., pp. 1097–99; and Ernst-Ulrich Petersmann, "International Competition Rules for the GATT-WTO World Trade and Legal System," *Journal of World Trade* (December 1993). This draft International Antitrust Code would establish minimum international standards. It is based on four principles: national laws should be used to solve international problems; national treatment; minimum standards; and international authority to settle disputes. It also includes standards for horizontal and vertical restraints.

Chapter 2

Labor Standards in International Trade: Do They Matter and What Do We Do About Them?

Dani Rodrik

Labor costs have always been a controversial issue in international trade policy. Every trade economist takes delight in demonstrating to a class of undergraduates the fallacy of the pauper-labor argument, one of the oldest and most durable arguments against free trade. Nonetheless, the idea that a comparative advantage based on low wages is unnatural and unfair has had great appeal throughout history. In 1892, the Republican Party platform went so far as to require import duties equal to the difference between wages abroad and at home to be levied on all imports competing with U.S. production.[1] To take a much more recent example, consider the following statement by an AFL-CIO representative:

> We spend a great deal of time talking about free trade and comparative advantages, and so forth, and I am sure these are important concepts and certainly we in the U.S. labor movement subscribe to them. Labor has benefited greatly from freeness and free trade, not only internationally, but domestically, from the comparative advantages that result from having a productive society as large and as diverse as we do in the United States, but the American labor movement has always taken the position that, *to the maximum extent possible, labor costs should be removed from that equation,* because labor is more than just a cost of production. Labor involves human dignity; it involves another whole dimension than does capital or interest or the other factors of production, and it therefore has to be treated very differently from them.[2] [emphasis added]

Although economists would think it folly that one should want to neutralize labor-cost differences in this way, the idea remains widely shared.

Most trade unionists and other labor representatives would now accept that wage differences based on labor-productivity differentials are legitimate and not cause for concern. The debate, therefore, has shifted to the area of labor-market policies, and more specifically, labor standards. It is alleged that exploitative practices in many low-wage exporting countries "artificially" depress labor costs, leading to unfair "competitive advantage" in world markets and a downward pressure on labor standards in rich countries. The practices most frequently cited include child labor, hazardous working conditions, absence of collective bargaining, and repression of labor unions. The Clinton administration had to persuade Mexico to sign side agreements on labor (and environment) before NAFTA could be sent to the U.S. Congress. Although the recently completed Uruguay Round of trade negotiations did not deal with labor standards, the issue is likely to be on the agenda (along with environment and competition policy) of any future set of multilateral trade talks. In some countries, pressure is building up for unilateral action as well.[3]

Trade economists respond to the clamor for labor standards by pointing out that there is very little economic rationale for the "upward" harmonization of labor standards. Countries with different sets of values and at different levels of income will naturally choose different labor-market policies. Where there exists prima facie evidence of exploitative practices, most trade economists would argue a combination of the following: 1) inadequate legislation and/or enforcement of labor standards is not a trade matter per se; 2) the appropriate manner in which to deal with such problems is through multilateral negotiations; and 3) trade restrictions or sanctions are likely to backfire by hurting precisely the groups they aim to protect.[4] One of the strongest weapons in the arsenal of the free trade camp is the argument that the advocates of labor standards are essentially protectionists and will use any argument that will help them obtain trade restrictions.[5]

There are few areas of trade policy where the gap between the two sides of the argument is so wide and apparently so unbridgeable. As Richard Freeman puts it,

> the argument about labor standards [is] one of a set of running battles between those
> who believe the unfettered market can do no wrong and those who believe govern-
> mental regulations can make things better. If you like standards, trot out the (usual)
> arguments about market imperfections, externalities, unequal bargaining power,
> prisoners' dilemma or coordination games, etc. If you don't like standards, trot out the
> (usual) arguments about the wonders of the Invisible Hand, the ineffectiveness of
> governments to act in the public interest, rent-seeking, etc. The debate is long on ide-
> ology and rhetoric and short on analysis and evidence.[6]

Taking Freeman's admonishment seriously, this paper aims to provide some fresh analysis and evidence. I will focus on three sets of issues in particular. First, to what extent should labor standards in the South be a matter of concern for trade policy in the North? Second, is there any hard evidence that labor standards affect trade and investment flows? Third, what are the implications for policy, especially regarding unilateral versus multilateral approaches.

As the issue is one that generates much heat, I should lay my cards on the table from the outset. As a trade economist, I am naturally in sympathy with the free traders' arguments on the dangers of opening the door to protectionist policies. And as an advocate for developing countries, I am especially concerned that upward harmonization in labor standards could rob these countries of some of their comparative advantage in labor-intensive goods. At the same time, I believe that some of the concerns that labor groups in advanced countries have over low labor standards in the developing world are justified and cannot be brushed away so easily. Such standards can appropriately become a matter for trade policy when they are viewed as unfair and exploitative by a wide segment of society in the importing country. In my judgement, the interests of the developing countries are better served by acknowledging the sources of resistance to some of their exports—and working around them—than by blithely repeating the free trade mantra.

· ·

ARE LABOR STANDARDS IN THE SOUTH A MATTER OF CONCERN FOR TRADE POLICY IN THE NORTH?

■ THE GATT/WTO SYSTEM has remained to date largely clear of labor-standard issues, the sole provision being one on prison labor in

Article XX(e) of the GATT. But the original International Trade Organization (ITO) Charter was more expansive on labor standards and trade. It had a whole article (Article VII) on fair labor standards, which stated that "all countries have a common interest in the achievement and maintenance of fair labor standards related to productivity and thus in the improvement of wages and working conditions as productivity may permit." Further: "unfair labor conditions, particularly in production for export, create difficulties in international trade, and, accordingly, each member shall take whatever action may be appropriate and feasible to eliminate such conditions within its territory." So these issues were very much in the minds of the architects of the postwar international economic system.

SOME PRELIMINARY DISTINCTIONS

It is useful to start with some distinctions to help get the issues focused. First, note that the question posed by this section's title is a narrow one: the issue is whether there is a case to be made for linkage between labor standards and *trade* policy, *not* whether labor standards in developing countries should be of concern to policymakers in the North. One can believe that industrial countries should be in the business of promoting human rights around the globe, without believing that trade policy has a role to play in it.

Second, and focusing on the labor standards/trade policy nexus proper, we must distinguish between two versions of the linkage. On the one hand, we have the argument that trade is a channel through which labor standards are arbitraged across countries toward the lowest level, requiring the use of trade policy to prevent a "race to the bottom." On the other hand, there is the argument that trade (and trade sanctions in particular) should be used to enforce internationally agreed standards such as ILO conventions, or to simply get trade partners to improve their labor standards. The two arguments are often mixed up, but the distinction is an important one analytically. The trade-as-sanction argument envisages the use of trade policy as a carrot and stick mechanism to get governments in developing countries to conform to labor market policies in the more advanced nations. This argument does not presume that labor standards in country A affect those in country B through trade; but it does presume that trade sanctions are appropriate and can be effective in obtaining compliance. For example, when President Reagan suspended Poland's most favored nation (MFN) status in October 1982, in part because of the banning of the independent trade union Solidarity, the linkage with trade was purely as a sanction. The race-to-the-bottom argument, on the other hand, does not presume that trade restrictions can get trade partners to alter their labor market policies, but it does presume that labor standards in the richer countries become harder to maintain as trade with low-standard countries intensifies. The NAFTA supplementary agreement on labor, for example, was clearly motivated by a desire to avoid a race to the bottom in the United States (although the mechanism envisaged in the agreement relies on improved enforcement of Mexico's own labor laws). As there is a fairly large literature on trade sanctions and their effectiveness, I will not have much to say about that here.[7]

Third, it is useful to reiterate the distinction already made in the introduction between low labor productivity, on the one hand, and inadequate legislation or enforcement of labor standards, on the other, in keeping labor costs low in poor countries. Most labor advocates would agree that only the latter is of concern, but their arguments often are not as careful on this front as one would wish. It is not uncommon to be told that nominal wages in India or China are some tiny fraction of wages in the United States as an argument for the unfairness of trade. Such wage comparisons are of course largely meaningless. Richard Freeman, for example, finds that around 80 percent of the variation in nominal wages among countries can be accounted for by the variation in two variables alone: educational composition of the work force and purchasing power of wages.[8] Later on, I will provide some direct evidence on the impact of labor standards proper on labor costs.

Finally, we should distinguish between labor-standard problems that arise from *uniformly* low standards in a trade partner, on the one hand, and those that arise from the *exemption* from national standards occasionally afforded to exporters, on the other. The latter is a common feature of export processing zones in developing countries. Steve Charnovitz cites a U.S. Department of Labor study that found that in five out of eleven nations looked at, labor rights in export processing zones were restricted in comparison to rights prevailing outside the zones.[9] As Charnovitz rightly argues, this could well be regarded as export subsidization and should be countervailable under GATT/WTO rules.

SOUTHERN LABOR STANDARDS, NORTHERN WAGES

Consider now the impact that labor standards—or lack thereof—in developing countries can have on labor markets in rich countries through international trade. Analytically, most cases of low labor standards can be thought of as an enlargement of the effective labor supply in the country concerned.[10] For concreteness, think of the employment of under-age children in manufacturing industries in the South. This increases the labor supply in the South by (roughly) the number of children added to the labor force as a consequence. For countries that already have a comparative advantage in unskilled labor-intensive industries such as clothing and footwear, this results in a strengthening of their comparative advantage. Southern exports of such products increase and northern imports must correspondingly increase as well. If collectively southern exporters amount to a large enough share of total supply—which is likely—the increase in import penetration in the North is achieved via a *fall* in the relative price of labor-intensive manufactures in world markets. The real wages of unskilled workers in the North are likely to decline as well, to the extent that southern exports compete head-on with northern production and northern production is also intensive in unskilled labor.

That much should be straightforward and uncontroversial. From this point on, the viewpoints diverge. To a trade economist, what has just transpired is the creation of gains from trade for the North. How? Essentially the North is now being offered goods at a cheaper price than before. The fall in the relative price of labor-intensive goods represents an *improvement* in the terms of trade of the North since the North is a net importer of such goods. To a first degree of approximation, the increase in the North's real income can be expressed as the product of the price reduction and the volume of net imports. While unskilled labor may lose, the North is richer as a whole, and if governments in the North wished to do so they could compensate the losers and still come out ahead.

To a labor advocate (and the average person on the street), however, things look very different. While the gains to other groups (and to all workers qua consumers) are undeniable, what has just happened is that unskilled workers in the North have been displaced from their jobs and their earnings reduced because of employment practices in the South that would be considered unconscionable in the North. While it would be nice if full compensation were to take place, it is extremely unlikely in practice.[11] Consequently, it is unfair that unskilled workers in the North should have to compete with child workers in the South and have to bear the costs for others' gains.

What is clearly at issue here is the *legitimacy* of the process through which net gains are being created in the North. The trade economist either prefers to ignore the process altogether, focusing on outcomes alone, or regards labor market institutions as a matter of national sovereignty and choice.[12] In either case, how comparative advantage is created in the South is of no consequence whatsoever to the North. The labor advocate is ready to moralize about process. But how do we distinguish legitimate moralizing from self-interested, self-serving advocacy?

In thinking about this issue, it helps to demystify international trade by recognizing that from the perspective of any individual country trade is *just like* an additional technology with which goods can be produced. In the domestic context, we think of a production function as representing the technology through which a set of intermediate inputs and primary factors is transformed into final goods. International trade is entirely analogous to such a production function: The goods that we sell abroad allow us to purchase imports in return, and hence our exports can be thought of as the inputs that get transformed into imports (the outputs). Prevailing international prices indicate the input-output coefficients used in this transformation. And, continuing the analogy, a terms-of-trade improvement (due, for example, to lower labor standards in a partner country) acts just like a technical advance in this technology, by reducing the input-output coefficients.

This is a helpful way of looking at trade because it raises the debate to a level that is potentially more conducive to constructive exchange. For one thing, this perspective clarifies that the opening up of new trade opportunities is no different from the kind of technological progress that governments routinely pursue and encourage, even when such progress has sharp distributional considerations. We would not dream of banning the electric bulb to please the candle makers!

At the same time, the analogy with technology clarifies a central issue: Nations do have collective preferences over what kinds of production technologies are admissible ("fair" or "legitimate"), and governments have always had restrictions on technologies that violate these boundaries, even on those that promise a large increase in a nation's productive potential. The ban on slave labor is, of course, the example that comes immediately to mind. But there are many, many more. Experimentation on human subjects, for example, is generally illegal, even when there is full consent and when the potential medical benefits from a discovery are large. Experiments on animals are heavily regulated, and there is much support for the idea of banning them altogether.[13] And, of course, over the last two centuries rich countries have developed labor legislation and standards that heavily circumscribe the nature of the production process. Making a new discovery by sheer hard work and ingenuity is applauded; making a new discovery by experimenting on (willing) human beings, paying workers below minimum wages, or using child labor is not.

The main point is that national laws and regulations always intrude on technology on grounds of fairness or legitimacy. It is difficult to see why a particular sort of technology, that which is embodied in international trade, should be immune from the same type of considerations.

One big difference is that the trade technology involves foreigners, and as such can become subject to an "us" versus "them" distinction. The Bangladeshi children, Chinese prisoners, or Indian women who labor under substandard conditions are not part of "our" community, and we may not feel it appropriate or practical to extend to them the protection that we provide our own workers. But once it is granted that the process by which goods are produced can be legitimately subject to regulation, the case for not interfering with trade because only foreigners are involved becomes one of degree and not of kind. Simple introspection will reveal that citizens of the rich countries are not utterly indifferent to the well-being of workers in other countries. As Richard Freeman reminds us, most of us would be willing to pay a few additional cents (if not a dollar or two) to buy a shirt that we knew was manufactured by foreign workers under safe and adequate working conditions.[14] Moreover, our willingness to pay for labor standards abroad is presumably even higher when standards in *our own* community as well would be otherwise affected negatively.

The following thought experiment may clarify the issues. Suppose an entrepreneur in a rich country announces that he has discovered a new proprietary technology that substantially lowers the cost of manufacturing garments. Workers using the old technology will most likely suffer losses as a result. On the other hand, aggregate national income will be increased, and consequently there is little reason for the government to interfere. Suppose, however, that the "invention" in question consists of the following: The entrepreneur has opened up a sweatshop and is importing child labor from abroad to manufacture garments. The economic consequences are of course the same as before, and there are still aggregate gains to the domestic economy. From a public policy standpoint, however, the situation now looks very different. There is first the well-being of the migrant foreign workers to take into account. There are circumstances under which this may not be an appropriate concern, say because these workers would have been even worse off not migrating. Still, we are unlikely to allow *domestic* workers to be adversely affected by the use of grossly substandard labor practices at home, even if such practices are limited to noncitizens. If that does not seem self-evident, note that very few advanced nations condone a substantially lower set of working conditions for migrant workers (temporary or otherwise). The reasons have less to do with humanitarian concerns for foreigners than with ensuring labor standards for *domestic* workers do not erode. The fact that this is hardly controversial points to the existence of a general social ethic that is at odds with the notion that free trade should prevail no matter what the state of labor standards in the partner countries. (Free trade with a low-standard country would be no different than importing workers from abroad and allowing them to work under the same poor conditions, as in the hypothetical example above.)

What I take from this is the following. There is no categorical case for exempting trade from the requirement that economic activities be based on processes that are generally viewed as fair and legitimate. The implication is that weak labor standards in trade partners cannot be presumed to be of no consequence for domestic trade policy. What this means for the conduct of actual trade policy, however, is not so clear. There are several thorny issues that need to be confronted: How do we know what is fair and legitimate? How can we truthfully elicit preferences in the importing countries on the valuation of higher standards in the South? What if the consequences of raising labor standards in the South are even worse than the consequences of low standards? And finally what is the exact role to be played by trade policy? These are difficult questions, but I would claim that they become easier to resolve when there is a shared understanding on the principles laid out above. I will return to these questions later.

IS THERE A RACE TO THE BOTTOM IN LABOR STANDARDS?

The previous discussion focused on the case where low labor standards in the South exert downward pressure on wages in the North. A more common complaint is that low labor standards create downward pressure on importing countries' labor standards as well. This is the well-known race-to-the-bottom argument, according to which workers in the North will have to acquiesce in standards that are low enough to prevent footloose capital and employers from deserting them for the South.

The argument has surface appeal but is correct only in a limited sense to be explained below. The case against it has been put well by Richard Freeman:[15] Any country that wants higher labor standards can purchase them for itself, regardless of the level of standards in other countries, in one of the following three ways. First, a currency devaluation can be used to reduce domestic costs in foreign currency terms, thereby offsetting the loss in competitiveness. Second, there could be a downward adjustment in wages directly. Third, the cost of higher labor standards can be paid for by the government and financed through an increase in taxes. Provided one or a combination of these approaches is followed, the presence of demanding labor standards does not put competitiveness and jobs at risk in the rich countries. The race to the bottom need not take place.

There is a sense, however, in which the race to the bottom becomes more likely as integration with low-standard countries increases. That is because increased trade and investment opportunities make it almost certainly more costly *for labor* to maintain high standards.

The point is best seen using the supply-demand framework in Figure 1. Let the initial labor-market equilibrium in the North be at A, with wages at w_0. Now consider the consequences of raising labor standards. From the perspective of employers, labor standards can be viewed as a tax on employment. The result is a shift up in the effective labor supply curve (as shown in the figure), by an amount corresponding to the additional (per-worker) cost of maintaining the standard. In the new equi-

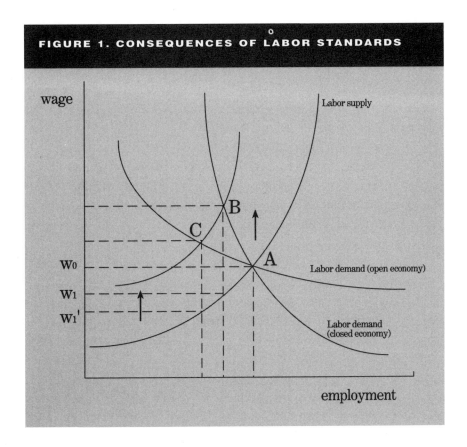

FIGURE 1. CONSEQUENCES OF LABOR STANDARDS

wage

Labor supply

B

C

w_0 — Labor demand (open economy)

w_1

w_1'

Labor demand (closed economy)

A

employment

librium, as in the usual tax-incidence analysis, some of the additional cost will be borne by employers and the rest by workers. What determines the distribution of the cost between employers and workers is the elasticity of demand for labor. Two cases are shown in the figure.

In an economy that is more open to foreign trade and investment, the demand for labor will generally be more elastic. The reason is that employers and the final consumers can substitute for foreign workers more easily—either by investing abroad or by importing the products made by foreign workers. The point is put graphically by a labor representative:

> the world has become a huge bazaar with nations peddling their work forces in competition against one another, offering the lowest prices for doing business. The customers, of course, are the multinational corporations.[16]

In the standard 2×2 Heckscher-Ohlin trade model (i.e., two goods and two factors of production), domestic labor demand is in fact perfectly elastic as long as there is incomplete specialization, even in the absence of foreign investment.[17] While one may not want to stretch these models too far, it stands to reason that openness to trade and foreign investment makes labor demand more elastic, and that an increase in such openness increases the elasticity of labor demand.

As Figure 1 shows, the more elastic is labor demand, the greater the part of the cost increase due to the labor standard that is borne by workers: Wages have to fall from w_0 to w_1', rather than from w_0 to w_1. The reduction in domestic employment is larger as well. Hence, in an integrated world economy, higher labor standards cost workers more, in terms of both wages and jobs.

Relating this result to the Freeman argument, it is still the case that higher labor standards can be maintained if there is a willingness to pay for them. What increased openness to trade and foreign investment does, however, is render it more difficult for workers to make other groups in society, and employers in particular, share in the costs. Consider the three options mentioned earlier: devaluation, taxation, and wage cuts. As long as employers and capitalists have the option of moving (or importing from) abroad, they cannot be induced to take a hit in terms of real after-tax earnings. Therefore, devaluation can work only insofar as it results in a disproportionate cut in take-home real wages. The same is true for taxation. One way or another, it is workers that must pay the lion's share of the cost.

It could be argued that this is appropriate insofar as it is *labor* standards, and hence an improvement in the working conditions for labor, that is at issue. Labor advocates, in turn, could point out that increased integration with poor countries is undoing a prevailing implicit bargain with employers.

. . . .

DO LABOR STANDARDS MATTER FOR TRADE AND INVESTMENT?

■ THERE IS NO UNIVERSAL, COMMON DEFINITION of labor standards, but such standards are usually thought to cover areas like child labor, working conditions, and collective bargaining. One useful taxonomy from Alejandro Portes is presented in Table 1.

TABLE 1. A TAXONOMY OF LABOR STANDARDS

I.	Basic Rights	Rights against use of child labor Rights against involuntary servitude Rights against physical coercion
II.	Survival Rights	Right to a living wage Right to accident compensation Right to a limited work week
III.	Security Rights	Rights against arbitrary dismissal Right to retirement compensation Right to survivors' compensation
IV.	Civic Rights	Right to free association Right to collective representation Right to free expression of grievances

Source: Alejandro Portes, "By-Passing the Rules: The Dialectics of Labour Standards and Informalization in Less-Developed Countries," in International Labour Standards and Economic Interdependence, *ed. Werner Sengenberger and Duncan Campbell (Geneva: International Institute for Labour Studies, 1994), Table 5*

The International Labour Organization's (ILO) conventions come perhaps closest to representing a universal set of labor standards. The membership of the ILO is composed of tripartite representatives from labor, employers' organizations, and governments. Since its first session in 1919, the ILO has approved no less than 174 conventions, of which 171 are considered to be in force.[18] (The remaining three, as of June 1, 1994, had not yet received the required number of ratifications to enter into force.) These range from the Hours of Work (Industry) Convention of 1919 to the Prevention of Major Industrial Accidents Convention of 1993. Once ratified by a member government, a convention has the force of law in the country concerned. In addition to these conventions, 181 recommendations, which are purely advisory, have been adopted. The ILO does not have enforcement power, and it relies on persuasion and voluntary compliance with ratified conventions. It does exercise a fair amount of monitoring and surveillance over the application of ratified conventions.

There is a great amount of variation in the ratification coverage of conventions by country. Oddly enough, the United States has ratified a very small number of conventions—11 in all, with the 1985 Labor Statistics Convention one of them—and stands as one of the laggards in this respect. India, meanwhile, has ratified 36, Iraq 64, Haiti 23, Cuba 86, and the Central African Republic 35. Some recent conventions that have not been ratified by the United States include: Night Work Convention (1990), Chemicals Convention (1990), Safety and Health in Construction Convention (1988), Asbestos Convention (1986), Occupational Health Services Convention (1985), Termination of Employment Convention (1982), and Occupational Safety and Health Convention (1981). Among other developed countries, the United Kingdom has ratified 80 Conventions, Japan 41, France 114, and Germany 73.[19]

It is clear that the number of conventions ratified is not, on its own, a good measure of the level of labor standards in a country. Nor does the ratification of a particular convention provide adequate information about compliance with a particular standard. Few would believe that workers are less likely to be exposed to asbestos in the workplace in

Cameroon—which has ratified the 1986 Asbestos Convention—than they are in the United States—which has not.

There is of course plenty of anecdotal evidence about lax standards in many developing countries. To obtain some rough quantitative feel for the disparities among countries and to see how different countries stack up against each other, it is useful to look at some statistical indicators that relate to labor standards. As a prelude to the empirical analysis that comes next, I will describe a number of these indicators here. Some of these are based on adherence to ILO conventions, while the rest are taken from other databases and deal with either specific legislation or actual practices. For data and sources, see Tables A1 and A2 in the appendix to this chapter.

TOTCONV. This indicator is simply the total number of ILO conventions ratified by a country. It ranges from 0 (the Gambia, Oman, Vanuatu) to 123 (Spain).

BWRCONV. Not all of the ILO conventions are regarded as equally central to labor standards. This indicator is the number of conventions ratified by a country among six of the conventions relating to basic worker rights: Conventions 29 (Forced Labor), 87 (Freedom of Association and Protection of the Right to Organize), 98 (Right to Organize and Collective Bargaining), 105 (Abolition of Forced Labor), 111 (Discrimination), and 138 (Minimum Age). It ranges from 0 to 6.

CIVLIB, PRIGHTS, DEMOC. CIVLIB and PRIGHTS are the Freedom House indicators of civil liberties and political rights, respectively.[20] Although these deal with human and political rights that go considerably beyond labor standards, one expects that they would also capture workers' rights of organization and self-expression. Indeed, the Freedom House checklist for civil liberties includes questions on the presence of free trade unions, effectiveness of collective bargaining, and freedom from exploitation by employers. Unlike the previous two indicators, these are based mostly on actual practice rather than formal obligations. As Freedom House puts it, "[we do] not mistake constitutional guarantees of human rights for those rights in practice."[21] CIVLIB and PRIGHTS are each measured on a scale of 1 to 7, with larger values indicating *fewer* rights. Since CIVLIB and PRIGHTS are highly correlated, it is convenient to combine the two into a synthetic indicator I call DEMOC, using a transformation due to Helliwell.[22] DEMOC ranges from 0 to 1, with 1 indicating a full set of civil and political rights.

CHILD. This is an indicator meant to capture the extent to which child labor is condoned. It is coded with the help of a U.S. Department of Labor survey based in turn on U.S. embassy and ILO reports.[23] For each country, the survey indicates whether there are inadequacies either in legislation or enforcement relating to standards on child labor. Problems with legislation refer to lack of child labor legislation or provisions in the legislation that do not meet ILO criteria. Problems in enforcement usually relate to lack of a sufficient number of inspectors to implement the child labor legislation. I use the following score: a country receives 0 if no problems are reported on either score, 1 if there is a problem with either legislation or enforcement, and 2 if problems are reported on both scores.

HOURS. This is the statutory hours of work in a normal working week, in manufacturing or construction (when no data on manufacturing is reported). It ranges from 40 to 48.

LEAVE. Days of annual leave with pay in manufacturing. It ranges from 5 (El Salvador, Sudan, and Tunisia) to 38 (Finland).

UNION. Percentage of the labor force that is unionized. It ranges from 1 percent to over 100 percent.

All of these indicators have their problems, but I have deliberately cast a wide net in the hope that collectively they may provide an accurate and useful picture. The detailed information on each country is reported in the appendix. Table 2 provides a matrix of correlations between the indicators, as well as their correlations with per-capita income (GDPSH589). The correlations are mostly in the expected direction. Hence, DEMOC, TOTCONV, LEAVE, and UNION are strongly positively correlated with per-capita income, while CHILD is strongly negatively correlated with it. High labor standards in one dimension tend to go with high standards in other dimensions, although the correlations are not always very strong, pointing to the need for using a diverse set of indicators. There are a few counterintuitive findings; for example, democracies seem to have longer working hours.

TABLE 2. CORRELATION MATRIX

	DEMOC	BWRCONV	TOTCONV	CHILD	HOURS	LEAVE	UNION	GDPSH589
DEMOC	1.00							
BWRCONV	0.22	1.00						
TOTCONV	0.40	0.65	1.00					
CHILD	-0.21	-0.07	-0.14	1.00				
HOURS	0.14	-0.18	0.17	0.12	1.00			
LEAVE	0.43	0.50	0.65	-0.37	-0.41	1.00		
UNION	0.28	0.33	0.31	-0.37	-0.19	0.47	1.00	
GDPSH589	0.67	0.12	0.39	-0.44	0.21	0.57	0.42	1.00

Source: See appendix.

EMPIRICAL EVIDENCE ON LABOR
STANDARDS AND TRADE

In this section, I use the indicators discussed above to look for evidence that labor standards—or lack thereof—have consequences for trade and foreign investment patterns. In line with the previous discussion, I will focus on three questions in particular: 1) Do labor standards affect labor costs? 2) Do labor standards affect comparative advantage, and thereby trade flows? and 3) Do labor standards affect foreign direct investment?

Labor costs are determined first and foremost by productivity. To see whether labor standards make a difference as well, I regress annualized labor costs in dollars (LABCOST) on per-capita income, to control for productivity,[24] and on the indicators of labor standards for which there are enough observations. (Data and sources are given in the appendix.) Table 3 reports the results. Unfortunately, the labor cost variable is available for less than 40 countries. Nonetheless, the results are interesting. Not surprisingly, per-capita income is strongly correlated with labor costs, as you would expect from the parallel between GNP per worker and GNP per capita.[25] But so are some of the labor indicators. The coefficients on BWRCONV and TOTCONV are both positive and statistically significant, as is the coefficient on DEMOC. The coefficient on CHILD is negative and often statistically significant at the 1 percent level. The small sample size notwithstanding—35 or 36 countries depending on the regression—these are fairly strong results, indicating that labor costs tend to increase as standards become more stringent.

Moreover, the estimated coefficients are large, implying that the economic magnitude of the effects are significant as well. For example, an increase of one step in our measure of child labor (going, say, from no child labor legislation to having such legislation) is associated with an increase in annual labor costs of $4,849–$8,710. These are very large numbers. Note, however, that child-labor practices are likely to be correlated with other shortcomings in labor standards. Consequently, what the parameter estimates are probably giving us is an indication of the aggregate effect of all of these.

Next we turn to comparative advantage. As discussed previously, the impact of labor standards is likely to be felt most strongly on labor-

TABLE 3. LABOR STANDARDS AND LABOR COSTS
(annual labor costs in U.S. dollars, 1985–88)

Independent Variables	Dependent Variable: LABCOST				
Constant	-4,685 (3,690)	1,596 (4,037)	3,205 (3,553)	-2,830 (4,691)	-1755 (4,865)
GNPCAP85	2.203* (0.265)	1.450* (0.331)	1.545* (0.308)	1.351* (0.327)	1.470* (0.335)
BWRCONV	1,707** (751.0)	2,524* (784.5)		1,736*** (889.0)	
TOTCONV			143.9* (3.720)		
CHILD		-8,710* (2,508)	-6,240* (2,272)	-6,965* (2,533)	-4,849*** (2,391)
DEMOC				9,968*** (5,813)	15,836* (5,197)
N	36	35	35	35	35
R²	0.71	0.78	0.79	0.80	0.77

Notes: See appendix for variable definitions. Standard errors are reported in parentheses.
*   significant at 1 percent level.
** significant at 5 percent level.
*** significant at 10 percent level.
Source: See appendix.

intensive goods. Consequently, I use as my dependent variable a measure of comparative advantage in labor-intensive goods: the ratio of textile and clothing exports to other exports, excluding fuels (TXTNTXT). I use the following two controls for the natural determinants of comparative advantage: population-to-land ratio (POPAREA85), which is a proxy for the labor endowment of a country relative to its land endowment and is expected to be positively correlated with TXTNTXT; and average years of schooling in the population aged over 25 (HUMAN85), which is a proxy for human capital and is expected to be negatively correlated with TXTNTXT.[26] The benchmark regression with just these two explanatory variables is shown in the first column of Table 4. The results indicate that these two variables are associated with comparative advantage in labor-intensive goods in the expected manner. The population-to-land ratio is positively associated with comparative advantage in textiles and clothing, and human capital is negatively associated with it. Although both parameter estimates are statistically significant, the overall fit of the equation is not as good as in the case of labor costs.

The other columns in Table 4 experiment with adding different combinations of labor standard indicators in the benchmark regression. With one exception, there are no statistically significant results. The exception is the regression including HOURS, which indicates that longer statutory hours are associated with a stronger comparative advantage in textiles and clothing. The signs on DEMOC and UNION are negative, but the parameter estimates are not statistically significant. The parameter estimate for CHILD is consistently positive and at times borderline significant (at the 10 percent level). Hence, while the pattern of signs is supportive of the hypothesis that low labor standards can help create comparative advantage in labor-intensive goods, the results are not very strong.

The sample of countries used for the regression in Table 4 includes both rich and poor nations. To see whether the presence of rich countries plays a confounding role, I have repeated the exercise after removing from the sample high-income countries, defined as countries with 1985 per capita GDP larger than $6,000. The results are reported in Table 5. We note first that the fit of the benchmark equation is now much improved, although still not extraordinary. In addition, we find that CHILD is statistically significant (with a positive sign) in a couple of the

TABLE 4. LABOR STANDARDS AND COMPARATIVE ADVANTAGE
(ratio of textile and clothing export to other exports, excluding fuels)

Dependent Variable: TXTNTXT

Independent Variables							
Constant	0.42* (0.11)	0.45** (0.20)	0.44* (0.12)	0.22*** (0.12)	-1.60** (0.80)	0.24 (0.17)	0.32** (0.13)
POPAREA85	1.13E-07** (4.50-08)	1.12E-07*** (5.74E-08)	1.55E-07 (2.42E-07)	1.57E-07 (2.40E-07)	1.92E-07 (2.54E-07)	4.29E-07*** (2.42E-07)	1.09E-07 (2.36E-07)
HUMAN85	-0.04* (0.01)	-0.04* (0.02)	-0.08 (0.03)	-0.02*** (0.01)	-0.08** (0.04)	-0.02 (0.02)	-0.03** (0.01)
BWRCONV		-0.01 (0.05)					
TOTCONV		0.00 (0.00)					
DEMOC			-0.11 (0.25)				
CHILD				0.14 (0.09)	0.15 (0.10)	0.15 (0.11)	0.06 (0.07)
HOURS					0.04** (0.02)		
UNION						-0.16 (0.17)	
LEAVE							0.00 (0.00)
N	84	84	83	83	54	46	36
R²	0.10	0.11	0.09	0.13	0.20	0.15	0.38

Notes: See appendix for variable definitions. Heteroskedasticity-consistent standard errors are reported in parentheses.
* significant at 1 percent level.   ** significant at 5 percent level.   *** significant at 10 percent level.
Source: See appendix.

TABLE 5. LABOR STANDARDS AND COMPARATIVE ADVANTAGE, EXCLUDING HIGH-INCOME COUNTRIES (ratio of textile and clothing exports to other exports, excluding fuels)

Independent Variables	Dependent Variable: TXTNTXT						
Constant	0.42*	0.44***	0.47*	0.19	-1.81**	0.28	0.28
	(0.11)	(0.24)	(0.12)	(0.15)	(0.73)	(0.27)	(0.23)
POPAREA85	1.43E-06**	1.54E-06**	1.54E-06**	1.50E-06*	1.57E-06**	7.92E-07	1.50E-06**
	(6.22E-07)	(6.35E-07)	(6.16E-07)	(5.36E-07)	(6.59E-07)	(4.80E-07)	(5.71E-07)
HUMAN85	-0.07**	-0.09**	-0.05	-0.06**	-0.10*	-0.04	-0.10*
	(0.03)	(0.03)	(0.04)	(0.03)	(0.03)	(0.05)	(0.03)
BWRCONV		-0.03					
		(0.07)					
TOTCONV		0.00					
		(0.00)					
DEMOC			-0.03				
			(0.30)				
CHILD				0.18***	0.14	0.18	0.15**
				(0.10)	(0.10)	(0.14)	(0.07)
HOURS					0.05*		
					(0.02)		
UNION						-0.44	
						(0.47)	
LEAVE							0.00
							(0.00)
N	56	56	56	56	49	30	17
R²	0.22	0.25	0.24	0.28	0.36	0.10	0.62

Notes: See appendix for variable definitions. Heteroskedasticity-consistent standard errors are reported in parentheses.
* significant at 1 percent level.   ** significant at 5 percent level.   *** significant at 10 percent level.

Source: See appendix.

regressions, along with HOURS as before. The signs on DEMOC and UNION are in the expected direction, although these variables are still not statistically significant. The restricted sample, therefore, provides somewhat stronger support for the idea that labor standards can influence comparative advantage.

The final set of empirical estimates focus on foreign direct investment (FDI), and these are shown in Table 6. The dependent variable in these regressions is the value of investment during 1982–89 by majority-owned U.S. affiliates abroad, normalized by the stock of such investment in the relevant countries at year-end 1982. I have selected the period 1982–89 for analysis because the last two available benchmark surveys undertaken by the U.S. Department of Commerce are those for 1982 and 1989. Since the theory of FDI is nowhere as complete as that for comparative advantage, we do not have a good empirical model to use as a reference. Therefore the benchmark regression, shown in column 1 of Table 6, takes an eclectic approach and includes the following three explanatory variables: the black-market premium for foreign currency (BMP6L) as a proxy for policy distortions, population (POP89), and income growth in host country (GROWTH82-89).[27] With the exception of population, there is a reasonable a priori prediction regarding the sign on these variables, and the expectations are borne out. Countries with low black-market premia and high growth receive more FDI.

As in the previous set of regressions, the other columns in the table report the results when the labor-standard indicators are introduced. In this case, we find statistically-significant relationships for DEMOC and CHILD. But these go in opposite directions from what one may have predicted. Countries with a lower democracy score and a higher CHILD score have received *less* foreign investment during 1982–89 than would have been predicted on the basis of other country characteristics. Taken at face value, these results indicate that low labor standards may be a hindrance, rather than an attraction, for foreign investors. One can speculate about the reasons for this findings. In particular, it is possible that DEMOC and CHILD are proxying for omitted country characteristics, leading to a bias for omitted variables. Nonetheless, it is interesting that the conventional wisdom about low-standard countries being a haven for foreign investors is far from being borne out.

TABLE 6. LABOR STANDARDS AND FOREIGN INVESTMENT

Dependent Variable: Manufacturing FDI by U.S. Majority-Owned Foreign Affiliates, 1982–89
(divided by the stock of FDI at year-end 1982)

Independent Variables				
Constant	0.03 (0.32)	-0.26 (0.62)	-1.46** (0.69)	0.19 (0.29)
BMP6L	-0.93** (0.42)	-0.73 (0.45)	-0.16 (0.51)	-0.31 (0.49)
POP89	-3.00E-09* (5.58E-10)	-3.05E-09* (6.37E-10)	-3.08E-09* (5.76E-10)	-2.88E-09* (5.23E-10)
GROWTH82-89	38.05* (10.43)	40.64* (11.51)	46.76* (11.35)	40.18* (10.53)
BWRCONV		-0.01 (0.14)		
TOTCONV		0.00 (0.01)		
DEMOC			1.44* (0.57)	
CHILD				-0.43** (0.20)
N	40	40	39	39
Adj. R²	0.53	0.51	0.57	0.55

Notes: See appendix for variable definitions. Standard errors are reported in parentheses.
* significant at 1 percent level.
** significant at 5 percent level.
*** significant at 10 percent level.

Source: See appendix.

To sum up, in view of the weakness of the data on labor standards and the difficulties involved in quantifying differences across countries on such a complex set of issues, I find the results overall suggestive. Indeed, I am rather surprised to have found any statistical regularities at all, even though the results on comparative advantage and on FDI tend to pull in opposite directions.

. . . .
HOW TO DEAL WITH LABOR STANDARDS

■ AT THIS POINT I ASSUME that we agree on two things: Labor standards can affect trade and foreign investment; and trade with low-standards countries does raise issues of legitimacy, fairness, and distributive justice. I now ask how we can move forward.

PRODUCT LABELING

One approach that is particularly appealing to an economist, and has been argued at length by Richard Freeman, is to use the market mechanism. Freeman draws an analogy between consumer demand for ordinary commodities and demand for higher labor standards:

> . . . a sizable proportion of citizens want some labor standards in their own country and also want some standards in the production of goods imported from other countries, just as they want TVs, doughnuts, or perfumes. Treating labour standards as a normal consumer good rather than as something extraneous to the economic system illuminates the underlying demand for standards. . . .[28]

But if there is a demand for standards, even for goods produced in foreign countries, *somebody* is going to be willing to supply them. If the Pakistani rug producer knows that he can charge a price premium for a rug "made by adult laborers working no longer than 8 hours a day," he will surely be willing to use such labor as long as the premium covers his additional labor costs. The trick is to get information about the production process in Pakistan to the final consumer in the United States. Labeling is the obvious solution. If imported goods can be appropriately labeled, consumers who are willing to pay a premium for higher standards in a foreign country will be able to do so. In turn, this will generate the incentive for producers in the exporting nations to upgrade their standards voluntarily.

Note how product labeling solves a number of problems. First, it allows the willingness-to-pay principle to dictate the extent of harmonization in labor standards. This is a great advantage insofar as it rules out uneconomic upgrading of standards in exporting countries. Second, it has the potential of making everyone better off without making anyone worse off: Consumers in the rich countries get the benefit of consuming products that are more in tune with their ethical concerns; poor-country exporters are compensated through higher prices for the costs of raising their labor standards; and import-competing workers in the rich countries get some natural protection through the higher prices. Third, labeling bypasses trade policy, does not require trade restrictions, and need not even involve any governmental action beyond perhaps setting some standards on labeling. This is important to anyone who distrusts government and bureaucracy. Finally, it prevents the labor-standards issue from being hijacked by protectionist groups.

Moreover, the idea of labeling is not pie in the sky; it is already happening. As a result of perceived pressure from consumers in rich countries, many companies have begun to declare their products friendly to (foreign) labor. Levi Strauss is probably the best known case. Following some unfavorable publicity in 1992 surrounding its use of underpaid workers in appalling conditions, Levi introduced new rules for its subcontractors and now excludes suppliers who use child labor or require very long working hours. One consequence was that the company had to stop importing from Myanmar and China. Following the broadcast of a videotape showing Bangladeshi children making shirts under contract, the giant retailer Wal-Mart was forced to follow Levi's example. Federated Department Stores, Inc., which owns Macy's, announced in April 1995 that it was pulling out of Myanmar for human-rights abuses. IKEA, the Swedish furniture store, recently announced that it would not sell carpets that it could not certify as having been made without child labor. A private European group has even launched a trademark—Rugmark—as a label that guarantees no child labor.[29] In all of these cases, the companies were obviously moved by their customers, a point that underscores the existence of a "demand" for labor standards. A British poll recently found that concerns over slavery and child labor now rank above the environment and animals.[30]

At the same time, it is important to recognize that labeling is only a partial solution to the problems raised by the concern over low labor standards. This is so for a number of reasons. First, labeling creates incentive problems for private firms. Since information about production conditions cannot be obtained costlessly, consumers cannot monitor the truth of the claims made in the labels. Firms consequently have the incentive to exaggerate the standards by which they abide. This appears to be a problem already. It was recently discovered that Levi Strauss is making use of 14–16-year-old girls in Bangladesh working up to 16 hours a day, contrary to its pledge mentioned previously.[31] These problems could be kept in check by close governmental monitoring, but this raises the specter of bureaucratic intrusion and protectionism once again. Second, the range of issues covered under the rubric of "labor standards" is so broad that it is difficult to see how simple labels could address all potential sources of worry. Even if labels could accurately signal whether child labor is employed or not, what about safety in the workplace? Hours of work? Nondiscrimination? Collective bargaining rights? That the ILO has more than 170 conventions reflects the multifaceted nature of labor standards.

The deeper objection to labeling is that we routinely reject labeling as a solution to similar concerns in the *domestic* setting. The logic of labeling applies equally well to domestic labor standards, yet we regard government mandated labor standards and regulations as perfectly appropriate domestically. For example, the reason there are regulations against asbestos in the workplace is that society as a whole presumably feels it is inappropriate to subject its labor force to hazardous conditions and is willing to pay for the higher costs that will result from the regulations. But in principle labeling would solve this domestic problem as well (or as badly) as it solves *foreign* labor-standard problems. If society is willing to pay for higher standards for its workforce, there would be demand for higher priced products labeled as "produced under nonasbestos conditions." Workers in turn could sort themselves into asbestos and nonasbestos plants, according to their risk preferences. That would be the obvious market-oriented solution; it would not require any government mandates and would have efficiency advantages over the regulatory approach.

Why then do most people not view the labeling approach as satisfactory in the domestic setting? Part of the answer has to do with the informational problems with labeling mentioned earlier. But note that such problems are probably less severe in the domestic context, where it is easier to observe work conditions in different companies. The more fundamental reason, I think, is that there are externalities in the demand for labor standards. My well-being is enhanced not just by my own "consumption" of higher labor standards, but also by my neighbors' consumption of the same. An extreme example helps make the point. Suppose slavery were legal, and there was an effective system of labeling. I would certainly be willing to pay more for goods not produced by slave labor. But I would also be willing to pay my neighbor something to get him not to buy slave-made goods. Or, as is even more likely, I would be willing to pay more for a house that is located in a town where no one buys slave-made goods. There are complicated ways in which labeling can deal with these demand-side externalities as well. One can imagine communities being built around shopping malls advertising "no slave-made goods sold here." But once the demand for labor standards is viewed as having a public element as well, the attractiveness of labeling is greatly weakened.[32] That is, I think, the main justification for having nationwide standards.

A SOCIAL-SAFEGUARDS CLAUSE?

Once it is granted that labor standards *can* be a trade issue, the question becomes the appropriate balance between multilateral and unilateral approaches. As a general principle, multilateralism is preferable to unilateralism in trade policy. Ideally, the way to proceed on labor standards would be through multilateral understandings such as those contained in ILO conventions. But the ILO is weak on enforcement and, as we have seen, there is less than universal adherence to most of its conventions. Such is the diversity of preferences among nations in this area that one should not expect much convergence on a common set of standards.[33]

However, what could be achieved multilaterally is a set of *rules governing the use of trade policy in connection with labor-standard issues.* We may think of this as the creation of a regime for social safe-guards. I have outlined elsewhere what such a regime might look like, and my discussion here will be based on this earlier work.[34]

As I discussed in the first part of the paper, restrictions on tech-nologies or market transactions that violate a widely held moral code are an established and accepted practice in domestic trade. There is little rea-son to believe that the attitude toward international trade would be any different. So I take it as axiomatic that no nation has to maintain free trade with a country or in a specific product if doing so would require *vio-lating a widely held ethical standard or social preference at home.* Such ethical or social opprobrium has to be shared widely within the importing country to justify trade restrictions. There are two immediate problems. First, how can we ensure that the social-safeguards principle is invoked only in cases where the violation involves a "widely held ethical standard or social preference." In other words, how do we prevent its derogation into standard protectionism? Second, what do we do in cases where its invocation results in a loss to a foreign trade partner (a developing coun-try in particular)? I take up each question in turn.

GUIDELINES FOR A SOCIAL-SAFEGUARDS CLAUSE

What we need is a procedure that tests for the validity of the moral claim by attempting to ascertain whether the values in question are held widely in the importing country or not. Consider the following pro-cedure. Any domestic producer, consumer, or public-interest group is allowed to bring a social-safeguards case before the domestic investigat-ing authority (the International Trade Commission, or ITC, in the United States), asking for import restrictions from the offending country. The authority is then required to solicit public testimony from all concerned parties, and in particular from retailers, consumer groups, and from a rep-resentative sample of exporters to the country concerned. These groups are asked to present their own views on the specific charge and on the likely effectiveness of the remedy being sought. After public debate and hearing all sides, the investigating authority finally reaches a judgment on 1) whether the specific charge has widespread public support, and 2) whether import restrictions are called for.

This procedure has a precedent of sorts in Article III:1 of the Uruguay Round Agreement on Safeguards, which says in part:

> A Member may apply a safeguard measure only following an investigation by the competent authorities of that Member. . . . This investigation shall include reasonable public notice to all interested parties and public hearings or other appropriate means in which importers, exporters, and other interested parties could present evidence and their views, including the opportunity to respond to the presentations of other parties and to submit their views, *inter alia*, as to whether or not the application of a safeguard measure would be in the public interest.

To serve the purposes of a social-safeguards clause, the requirements stated above should be strengthened in a number of directions. First, there should be an explicit mention of domestic retailers, distributors, and consumer groups, alongside exporters, as the parties whose views should be sought. Second, the investigating authority should *require* testimony from such groups, rather than simply allowing it as in the present text. Third, it should be made clear that the investigating authority has two questions to resolve: Is the labor-standard concern on which the complaint is based one that is also shared by groups whose material interests would be adversely affected by trade restrictions? If the answer is yes, does the proposed remedy (i.e., trade restriction) fulfill an objective consistent with the standard in question? The authority would authorize trade action only when the answer to both questions is yes.

The suggested procedure has a number of advantages. First, note that by compelling testimony from groups who would be adversely affected by trade restrictions (retailers and exporters in particular), the process would make it difficult for groups competing with imports to present their self-interest as the public interest.[35] On the other hand, the public nature of the investigation should discourage purely opportunistic behavior by groups who would be harmed by trade restrictions. When widely held social and moral principles are at stake, it is unlikely that such groups would deny the strength of the case for the simple reason that their own legitimacy in the public's eye would be thrown in doubt. For example, we can hardly imagine an exporting industry association professing that there is nothing wrong with slavery, or a particularly egregious form of child labor. So soliciting the views of such groups should be an adequate test of the validity of the case for social safeguards. Another useful test would be to allow social safeguards cases to be brought *only* for a standard the importing country itself has accepted (say one of the ILO conventions).[36]

More often than not, of course, retailing and exporting interests will disagree with the industries competing with imports. The disagreement can center either on the moral issues, or on the efficacy of the trade remedy. We can visualize exporting groups arguing, for example, that low standards in, say, Bangladesh are not necessarily morally objectionable since poverty places limits on the stringency of standards. Or that stringent child-labor regulations may put children more at risk by throwing them into even more hazardous activities like prostitution.[37] We can also envisage a public debate—as happened during the recent renewal of China's MFN status in the United States[38]—on whether trade restrictions are an acceptable way of discharging a nation's moral or ethical obligations. In both cases, the process would be doing its job appropriately, distinguishing legitimate ethical and environmental concerns from pure protectionist chaff.

COMPENSATING COUNTRIES ADVERSELY AFFECTED BY SOCIAL SAFEGUARDS

Under the GATT 1994 safeguard rules, the country applying the safeguard is expected to "endeavor to maintain a substantially equivalent level of concessions and other obligations to that existing under GATT 1994 between it and the members that would be affected by such a measure" (Article VIII:1). If adequate compensation is not offered, affected exporting countries are free to retaliate by suspending some of their concessions or obligations to the importing country. Developing countries should naturally seek to extend these principles to the area of social safeguards as well. In addition, they should seek to strengthen the requirement of compensation.

The issue of compensation is likely to be a controversial one. Governments of developed countries can argue that countries that exploit their workers should not be allowed to profit from these acts and do not deserve compensation for trade restrictions imposed on them. Developing countries *with reasonably democratic regimes* would be on strong grounds in rejecting this argument. In such countries, the prevailing labor and environmental standards can be taken to reflect *prima facie* their own principles and priorities. It is a reasonable principle that nations should not be made to suffer for having made, in broadly democratic fashion, institutional choices that differ from those in the advanced industrial countries. As U.S. Labor Secretary Robert Reich has put it,

> . . . the existence of democratic institutions—multiple parties, freedom of speech and the press, clean elections—makes it more likely that low wages and poor working conditions are caused by unfortunate but legitimate economic constraints. The less democratic is a country, conversely, the greater the grounds for suspicion that labor standards are being suppressed to serve narrow commercial interests or a misguided mercantilist impulse on the part of elites. . . .
>
> Where there are reasonably robust democratic institutions, then, we can presume that labor conditions reflect what the country can afford, given its level of development.[39]

Authoritarian regimes cannot make the claim that their labor standards are reflective of broad social preferences. These standards may well be consistent with social preferences of course, but there is no *prima facie* case that they will be. Consequently, the case for compensating such countries is considerably weaker.[40] What is or is not a full democracy can of course be highly subjective. But in practice there are likely to be few cases in which the question of whether a country is "broadly democratic" would be seriously at issue.

The proposed procedure on "social safeguards" is summarized in Figure 2 in the form of a decision tree. The tree specifies the conditions under which trade restrictions would be allowed and compensation provided.

. . . .
CONCLUDING REMARKS

■   THE MAIN ARGUMENT OF THIS PAPER has been the following: By recognizing that individuals and nations have preferences not only

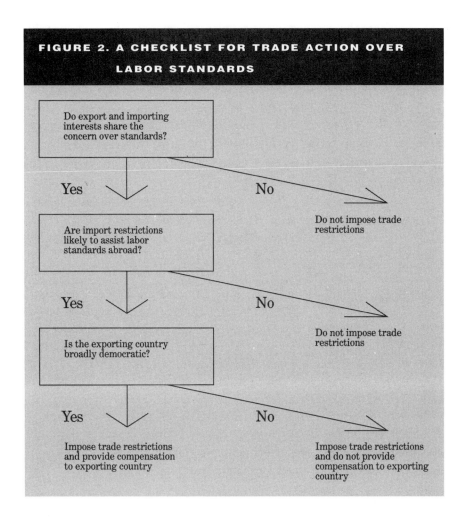

FIGURE 2. A CHECKLIST FOR TRADE ACTION OVER LABOR STANDARDS

Do export and importing interests share the concern over standards?

Yes

No → Do not impose trade restrictions

Are import restrictions likely to assist labor standards abroad?

Yes

No → Do not impose trade restrictions

Is the exporting country broadly democratic?

Yes → Impose trade restrictions and provide compensation to exporting country

No → Impose trade restrictions and do not provide compensation to exporting country

over outcomes (their "consumption bundle") but over the processes through which these outcomes are generated,[41] we can start bridging the gap that separates labor advocates from trade economists. International trade can be viewed as just another technology that promises to expand the size of the economic pie, possibly at some cost to certain individuals or groups. All governments take into account considerations of fairness and legitimacy in their regulations governing which technologies are admissible and which are not. The concern over labor standards is just another manifestation of this principle.

From the perspective of developing countries the main message of this paper is: Do not worry about pressure on labor standards per se, but worry about protectionism that masquerades under the guise of a quest for improved labor standards. The former is not necessarily an indication of the latter and should not be confused with it.[42] Once one is willing to believe that there is a valid distinction between these two, it becomes possible to design institutions that can respond to legitimate concerns in the North without undercutting the South's comparative advantage in labor-intensive products.

I have suggested, in particular, that an appropriately designed social-safeguards clause is worth serious consideration. The key is to ensure that the process is transparent and open to those groups— exporters, consumers, and retailers—whose interests are aligned with an open trade regime. Provided broad representation can be achieved, a social-safeguards process at home can be a useful mechanism for eliciting social preferences over labor standards in trade partners. Developing countries should have little to fear from such a mechanism.

There is of course a risk in instituting a social-safeguards clause. But there is also a risk in not doing so: Increasing domestic pressures on labor (and environmental) matters will lead to a new set of grey-area protectionist measures because there are no internationally agreed rules to channel these pressures into less harmful directions. If that happens, the consequences will be more damaging to developing-country interests than those of a social-safeguards clause negotiated multilaterally.

APPENDIX

TABLE A1. LIST OF VARIABLES AND SOURCES

Variable	Definition	Source
TOTCONV	Number of ILO Conventions ratified	WBLMDB
BWRCONV	Number of ILO Conventions ratified among Conventions 29, 87, 98, 105, 111, 138	computed from ILO, *Lists*
CIVLIB	Civil liberties index	Barro and Lee, from original source in Freedom House
PRIGHTS	Political rights index	Barro and Lee, from original source in Freedom House
DEMOC	Democracy index	computed from Barro and Lee, from original source in Freedom House
CHILD	Child labor indicator	computed from USDL
HOURS	Statutory weekly hours of work in manufacturing, 1983	WBLMDB, from original ILO source
LEAVE	Statutory days of annual leave in manufacturing, 1990	WBLMDB, from original ILO source
UNION	Percentage of the labor force that is unionized, 1983	WBLMDB
LABCOST	Labor cost per worker in manufacturing, in U.S. dollars per year, 1985–88	WBLMDB, from original ILO source
GDPSH585	Per capita GDP, 1985	Barro and Lee, from Summers-Heston
TXTNTXT	Ratio of textile and clothing exports (SITC 26+65+84) to other exports, excluding fuels, 1985	computed from HITDS and WBWT
POPAREA85	Population divided by land area, 1985	computed from WBWT
HUMAN85	Average years of schooling in above-25 population, 1985	Barro and Lee

(continued on next page)

Variable	Definition	Source
BMP5L	Log of one plus the black-market premium for foreign currency, 1980–84	Barro and Lee
WARDUM	Dummy for countries that have been involved in at least one war during 1960–1985	Barro and Lee
POP85	Population, 1985	WBWT
DETEXP85	Debt-export ratio, 1985	WBWDT

Key to sources:

Barro and Lee: Robert J. Barro and Jong-Wha Lee, "Data Set for a Panel of 138 Countries," unpublished paper, 1994.

Freedom House: Freedom in the World: The Annual Survey of Political Rights and Civil Liberties 1993–1994 *(New York: Freedom House, 1994).*

HITDS: UNCTAD, Handbook of International Trade and Development Statistics *(Geneva: UNCTAD, 1990).*

ILO, Lists: International Labour Office, Lists of Ratification by Convention and by Country, *Report III (part 5) (Geneva: ILO, 1994).*

Summers-Heston: R. Summers and A. Heston, The Penn World Tables, *database.*

WBLMDB: World Bank Labor Market Data Base, World Bank, Washington, DC, various years.

WBWDT: World Bank, World Debt Tables *(Washington, DC: World Bank, 1985).*

WBWT: World Bank, World Tables *(Baltimore, MD: Johns Hopkins University Press, 1985).*

USDL: United States Department of Labor, Foreign Labor Trends: International Child Labor Problems *(Washington, DC: Bureau of International Labor Affairs, 1992).*

Country	DEMOC	BWRCONV	TOTCONV	CHILD	HOURS	LEAVE	UNION
Afghanistan	0.03	2	15	1			
Algeria	0.25	6	52	1	44	20	0.175
Argentina	0.88	5	66	1	48		0.28
Australia	1.00	5	51	0			
Austria	1.00	5	47	1	48	20	1.202
Bahamas	0.78	3	26	0	48	27	0.25
Bahrain	0.33	1	4	0	48		
Bangladesh	0.42	5	31	2	48		
Bardados	0.98	5	35	0	40	20	0.32
Belgium	1.00	6	83	0		18	0.7
Benin	0.00	5	18	1	40	15	0.75
Bolivia	0.73	5	43	2	48		
Botswana	0.77	0	2	2	45		
Brazil	0.80	4	71	1	48		
Burkina Faso	0.13	4	31	1		12	
Burundi	0.10	4	23	1	45		0.45
Cameroon	0.15	5	47	0	40		0.306
Canada	1.00	3	27	0			
Cape Verde	0.22	4	9	1			
Central African Republic	0.13	5	35	1	40		0.01
Chad	0.05	5	18	1	40		0.2
Chile	0.37	2	41	1	48		
China	0.13	0	17	1			
Colombia	0.70	5	50	1	48	15	

(continued on next page)

Country	DEMOC	BWRCONV	TOTCONV	CHILD	HOURS	LEAVE	UNION
Comoros	0.18	4	29	0	40		
Congo	0.08	2	17	1	40		
Costa Rica	1.00	6	47	2	48	10	0.151
Côte d'Ivoire	0.23	5	31	1	40		0.2
Cyprus	0.93	5	43	1			
Denmark	1.00	5	61	0	40	25	0.65
Dominica	0.85	6	20	1	44		0.25
Dominican Republic	0.83	5	26	1	40		0.12
Ecuador	0.78	5	56	2	40		0.15
Egypt	0.43	5	59	2	48		
El Salvador	0.62	1	6	0	44	5	0.15
Ethiopia	0.03	3	15	1	48		
Fiji	0.53	4	17	1	47		
Finland	0.90	6	85	0		38	0.8
France	0.92	6	114	0		25	0.2
Gabon	0.17	5	34	0	40		
Gambia	0.67	0	0	1			0.275
Germany	0.93	6	70	0		30	
Ghana	0.13	5	45	1	45		0.13
Greece	0.85	6	65	1		22	0.175
Grenada	0.85	3	25	1			0.2
Guatemala	0.63	6	63	1	48		
Guinea	0.12	5	53	1	40		1

(continued on next page)

Country	DEMOC	BWRCONV	TOTCONV	CHILD	HOURS	LEAVE	UNION
Guinea-Bissau	0.12	4	30	1	48		
Guyana	0.35	5	40	1	48		0.34
Haiti	0.22	5	23	1	48		
Honduras	0.75	6	20	1	44	10	
Hungary	0.42	4	52	0			0.5
Iceland	1.00	5	18	0			0.6
India	0.75	2	36	1	48	17	0.05
Indonesia	0.28	2	10	1	40		0.05
Iran	0.25	3	11	0	48		
Iraq	0.02	5	64	1	48		0.1
Ireland	1.00	5	59	0			0.58
Israel	0.83	6	44	1	47		0.9
Italy	1.00	6	102	1		31	0.425
Jamaica	0.80	5	25	2	40		0.24
Japan	1.00	3	40	0		8	0.29
Jordan	0.32	4	17	1		18	0.1
Kenya	0.20	4	46	2	48		
Korea	0.57	0	3	0		8	0.234
Kuwait	0.32	4	14	0	48		
Lesotho	0.27	3	11	2	45	12	
Liberia	0.32	5	20	0	48		0.02
Luxembourg	1.00	5	66	0	48		
Madagascar	0.33	3	30	1	40	18	0.04

(continued on next page)

TABLE A2. INDICATORS OF LABOR STANDARDS (CONTINUED)

Country	DEMOC	BWRCONV	TOTCONV	CHILD	HOURS	LEAVE	UNION
Malawi	0.08	2	23	1	48		
Malaysia	0.47	3	23	0	48		
Mali	0.12	5	21	1	40	19	
Malta	0.83	6	56	0			0.4
Mauritania	0.12	3	37	1	40		
Mauritius	0.83	4	32	1	45		0.35
Mexico	0.53	4	74	1	48		0.35
Morocco	0.43	4	40	2	48		0.05
Mozambique	0.08	3	11	0	48		
Nepal	0.55	4	4	2		18	
Netherlands	1.00	6	92	0		32	0.29
New Zealand	1.00	3	56	0		15	
Nicaragua	0.33	4	58	1	48		0.35
Niger	0.10	6	30	1	40		
Nigeria	0.23	4	28	2	44		
Norway	1.00	6	97	0		21	
Oman	0.17	0	0	0			
Pakistan	0.52	5	30	1	48		0.1
Panama	0.30	5	69	1	48		
Papua New Guinea	0.83	3	19	0	44		
Paraguay	0.32	5	34	2	48		
Peru	0.73	5	66	1	48	18	0.02
Philippines	0.72	4	23	1	48		

(continued on next page)

Country	DEMOC	BWRCONV	TOTCONV	CHILD	HOURS	LEAVE	UNION
Poland	0.35	6	76	1			
Portugal	0.92	5	65	1	45	22	0.55
Rwanda	0.17	5	25	0	48	15	
Saudi Arabia	0.08	3	13	1	40		
Senegal	0.58	5	34	1	45		
Seychelles	0.17	3	19	0	44		
Sierra Leone	0.32	5	33	2	44		0.35
Singapore	0.43	3	21	1			
Solomon	0.85	1	14	2			
Somalia	0.00	3	14	1	48		
South Africa	0.25	0	12	2			0.17
Spain	0.93	6	123	1	48	22	
Sri Lanka	0.55	4	29	0			0.3
St. Lucia	0.92	2	25	1			0.2
St. Vincent	0.88	0	0				0.1
Sudan	0.28	4	12	2	48	5	
Suriname	0.45	3	26	0	48		
Swaziland	0.25	5	31	1	48		0.1
Sweden	1.00	6	83	0		25	
Switzerland	1.00	4	50	0		24	0.2
Syria	0.07	1	46	2	48		0.05
Tanzania	0.17	3	38	2	45		0.15
Thailand	0.67	2	11	2	48		

(continued on next page)

TABLE A2. INDICATORS OF LABOR STANDARDS (CONTINUED)

Country	DEMOC	BWRCONV	TOTCONV	CHILD	HOURS	LEAVE	UNION
Togo	0.17	5	19	0	40		
Trinidad	0.97	5	12	1		14	
Tunisia	0.33	5	55	2	48	5	0.2
Turkey	0.62	4	28	1	43		0.1
Uganda	0.38	3	25	2	48		
United Arab Emirates	0.32	1	4	2			
United Kingdom	1.00	5	80	1		25	0.357
United States	1.00	1	11	0		12	
Uruguay	0.85	5	97	1	48		
Vanuatu	0.68	0	0				
Venezuela	0.90	6	52	1	48	15	0.32
Western Samoa	0.63	0	0	1			
Yemen	0.33	1	26	1	48	18	
Yugoslavia	0.30	5	75	0			
Zaire	0.05	2	30	1	48		
Zambia	0.30	4	38	1	48	5	
Zimbabwe	0.30	0	5	0	46	16	0.17

Sources: See Table A1.

Notes

I am grateful to Jagdish Bhagwati, Ron Findlay, Catherine Gwin, Jim Hines, Robert Lawrence, Carlos Primo Braga, Sidney Weintraub, John Whalley, and Adrian Wood for comments. Chi Yin has provided excellent research assistance. The views expressed here are solely my own.

[1] Steve Charnovitz, "Fair Labor Standards and International Trade," *Journal of World Trade Law*, Vol. 20, No. 1 (January/February 1986), note 44.

[2] David W. Leebron, "Lying Down with Procrustes: An Analysis of Harmonization Claims," Working Paper No. 111 (New York: Center for Law and Economic Studies, Columbia University School of Law, January 1995), note 67.

[3] The United States has a history of introducing labor-standards criteria in its trade legislation. The 1983 Caribbean Basin Initiative, a program that eliminates tariffs on most products from Caribbean nations, requires for eligibility that workers be afforded "reasonable workplace conditions and enjoy the right to organize and bargain collectively." In the 1984 extension of the Generalized System of Preferences (GSP), beneficiaries were required to take steps to afford "internationally recognized working rights." See Charnovitz, "Fair Labor Standards," op. cit., for a discussion. GSP privileges have been removed from a number of countries on account of labor-standard violations.

[4] This does not imply that most trade economists are unconcerned about the moral or philosophical dimensions of the problem. One of the most complete analyses of these issues has been undertaken by Jagdish Bhagwati in Bhagwati and R. Hudec (eds.) *Fair Trade and Harmonization: Prerequisites for Free Trade?* (Cambridge, MA: MIT Press, 1996), Ch. 1. However, Bhagwati's position is that the lack of universal agreement on what constitutes appropriate standards rules out the inclusion of labor-standard considerations in trade policy formulation.

[5] For statements from two distinguished economists, see the contributions by Jagdish Bhagwati and T. N. Srinivasan in *International Labor Standards and Global Economic Integration: Proceedings of a Symposium* (Washington, DC: Bureau of International Labor Affairs, July 1994).

[6] Richard Freeman, "A Hard-Headed Look at Labour Standards," in *International Labour Standards and Economic Interdependence*, ed. Werner Sengenberger and Duncan Campbell (Geneva: International Institute for Labour Studies, 1994), p. 80.

[7] See, for example, Gary C. Hufbauer and Jeffrey J. Schott, *Economic Sanctions Reconsidered* (Washington, DC: Institute for International Economics, 1990).

[8] Richard Freeman, "A Global Labor Market? Differences in Wages Among Countries in the 1980s," unpublished paper, July 1994.

[9] Steve Charnovitz, "Environmental and Labour Standards in Trade," *The World Economy*, Vol. 15, No. 3 (May 1992), p. 343.

[10] For a useful analytical exposition on this, see Drusilla Brown, Alan Deardorff, and Robert Stern, "International Labor Standards and Trade: A Theoretical Analysis" (Ann Arbor, MI: University of Michigan, July 1993).

[11] For a careful evaluation of the difficulties in compensating workers hurt by import competition, see Louis Jacobson, "Evaluating Policy Responses Aimed at Reducing the Costs to Workers of Increased Import Competition," paper prepared for the Brookings Conference on Imports, Exports, and the American Worker, December 1994.

[12] See, for example, T. N. Srinivasan, "International Trade and Labour Standards" (New Haven, CT: Yale University, May 1995), unpublished paper.

[13] I owe the examples of human and animal experimentation to Ron Findlay in a personal communication.

[14] Freeman, op. cit.

[15] Ibid.

[16] Statement by Thomas R. Donahue in *International Labor Standards and Global Economic Integration*, op. cit.

[17] For a nice exposition, see Edward Leamer, "A Trade Economist's View of U.S. Wages and 'Globalization,' " unpublished paper, January 1995.

[18] Among these, 29 have been revised by a subsequent convention, and 26 are no longer open to ratification due to entry into force of a revising convention.

[19] The information in this paragraph is obtained from International Labour Office, *Lists of Ratification by Convention and by Country*, Report III, part 5 (Geneva: ILO, 1994).

[20] Freedom House, *Freedom in the World: The Annual Survey of Political Rights and Civil Liberties 1993–1994* (New York: Freedom House, 1994).

[21] Ibid., p. 673.

[22] John F. Helliwell, "Empirical Linkages Between Democracy and Economic Growth," *British Journal of Political Science*, Vol. 24 (1994), pp. 225–48. DEMOC=(14- (CIVLIB+ PRIGHTS))/12.

[23] United States Department of Labor, *Foreign Labor Trends: International Child Labor Problems* (Washington, DC: Bureau of International Labor Affairs, 1992).

[24] I also included an educational variable to control for the skill level of the work force, but it turned out that this variable was insignificant when per capita GNP was included. Using GNP per worker instead of GNP per capita in these regressions made no difference to the results.

[25] Ibid.

[26] The use of these proxies for relative factor endowments is inspired by the work of Kersti Berge and Adrian Wood, "Exporting Manufactures: Trade Policy or Human Resources?" IDS Working Paper No. 4 (Sussex, UK: Institute of Development Studies, University of Sussex, 1994).

[27] I thank Jim Hines for helpful discussions on the FDI data. The benchmark specification here is influenced by his paper "Forbidden Payment: Foreign Bribery and American Business After 1977" (Cambridge, MA: Harvard University, September 1995).

[28] Freeman, "Hard-Headed Look," op. cit.

[29] These examples are reported in *The Economist*, 3 June 1995, pp. 58–9.

[30] Ibid., p. 58.

[31] Ibid., p. 59.

[32] Freeman recognizes this: "But to the extent that consumers care about the existence of substandard conditions per se, regardless of whether they buy the goods so produced, legal enactment has an advantage [over labeling]." See Freeman, "Hard-Headed Look," op. cit.

[33] As Jagdish Bhagwati has concluded, "[t]he alleged claim for the universality of labour standards is . . . generally unpersuasive." See his "Trade Liberalization and 'Fair Trade' Demands: Addressing the Environmental and Labour Standards Issues," *The World Economy* (forthcoming 1995).

[34] See Dani Rodrik, "Developing Countries After the Uruguay Round," in UNCTAD, *International and Monetary Issues for the 1990s*, Vol. VI (New York: United Nations, 1995).

[35] This is one of the most important shortcomings of antidumping procedures in the United States. The law does not require that consumer or exporters views be heard or taken into account.

[36] This suggestion was made by Dave Richardson. This requirement would put the United States in an awkward corner as it has ratified few ILO conventions.

[37] *The Economist* (3 June 1995), p. 59 article cited previously reports: "Caroline Lequesne of Oxfam, a British charity, has just returned from Bangladesh, where she visited factories to determine the impact of American retailers' human-rights policies. She reckons that between 1993 and 1994, around 30,000 of the 50,000 children working in textile firms in Bangladesh were thrown out of factories because suppliers feared losing their business if they kept the children on. But the majority of these children have, because of penury, been forced to turn to prostitution or other industries like welding, where conditions pose far greater risks to them."

For a discussion of how the imposition of advanced labor standards in developing countries frequently gives rise to the emergence of an informal sector, see Alejandro Portes, "By-Passing the Rules: The Dialectics of Labour Standards and Informalization in Less Developed Countries," in Sengenberger and Campbell, op. cit.

[38] The fact that this debate actually took place is no guarantee that it will always do so. China is an important trade partner, and U.S. exporters rallied to the cause for fear of losing an important market. But suppose the country in question had been Bangladesh instead. Would there have been as much public debate? Probably not. Hence a major advantage of the proposed procedure is that it *forces* the debate to take place, even when the foreign country is a relatively small player in world markets, as most developing countries individually are.

[39] Keynote speech from a symposium sponsored by the Bureau of International Labor Affairs, U.S. Department of Labor, Washington, DC, July 1994.

[40] For a good discussion on this issue from the standpoint of environmental standards, see Richard Cooper, "Natural Resources and Environmental Policies" (Cambridge, MA: Harvard University Press, 1993).

[41] Amartya Sen has recently provided a good discussion of the issue: "[C]an we have sensible outcome judgements in a totally procedure-independent way? Classical utilitarianism does indeed propose such a system, but it is hard to be convinced that we can plausibly judge any given utility distribution ignoring *altogether* the process that led to that distribution (attaching, for example, no intrinsic importance whatever to whether a particular utility redistribution is caused by charity, or taxation, or torture)" [emphasis in the original]. Amartya Sen, "Rationality and Social Choice," *American Economic Review* (March 1995), p. 12.

[42] Alan Krueger has recently provided some interesting evidence on this point. Looking at the composition of sponsorship for the proposed Child Labor Deterrence Act of 1995—which, if passed, would prohibit the importation into the United States of goods produced using child labor—he found that representatives from districts with a high concentration of less-skilled labor were significantly *less* likely to be sponsors of the bill. This evidence runs against the belief that the concerns about child labor are primarily motivated by protectionist desires. See Alan Krueger, "Observations on International Labor Standards and Trade," unpublished paper, Princeton University, Princeton, NJ, April 1996.

Chapter 3

Trade and Environment, the WTO, and the Developing Countries

John Whalley

The trade and environment link has become a high profile issue in both communities in the last few years.[1] In reality, there is no single issue, but instead a series of interrelated dilemmas that have agglomerated to fuel a continuing debate. This paper looks at the linkage between trade and environment explicitly from the developing-country point of view.

At one level, the controversy over the trade and environment linkage derives from the contention by some in the environmental community that increased trade inevitably implies increased consumption and production and hence, lowered environmental quality. This theme was reflected in congressional debates on NAFTA, as it went through its various stages in 1991 and 1992, and focused on extreme environmental problems in the maquiladora free trade zone close to the U.S. border in Mexico. These included large untreated discharges into rivers, high infection rates in U.S. border communities attributed to shared U.S.-Mexican aquifers, and other related problems that were seen as inevitably worsening under NAFTA, with yet more U.S.-Mexican trade.[2] Under this view of the world, expanded trade and environmental quality are seen as being in direct conflict.

However, others involved in the debate see as overly simplistic the view that environmental worsening necessarily follows from increased trade. The GATT annual report for 1992 argued that the gains achieved through increased trade will increase real incomes; if these income gains are spent on environmental protection, higher rather than lower environmental quality may be the result. Moreover, when developing countries with outward-oriented trade policies are compared to those with less open policies (such as Korea compared with, for instance, India up to the late 1980s), the former seem to have achieved the improved environmental standards. In part, this is due to their need to sell into upper income markets with higher standards, which has required them to produce to higher environmental standards. In achieving high growth rates for significant periods of time and increased living standards, these same countries also seem to have witnessed a clear positive impact on environmental quality. This reflects, in part, the income elasticity of their own demand for environmental quality. Finally, these participants in the debate note that in the Organisation for Economic Co-operation and Development (OECD) countries, standards for air and water quality are considerably higher today than they were 50 years ago even though these same economies now trade considerably more as a percentage of GDP than before. This is, again, due to higher incomes and a positive income elasticity of demand for environmental quality.

A different aspect of the debate on the trade and environment issue revolves around the argument that environmental problems are now so serious that we cannot allow new and much needed environmental policy to be thwarted by concerns over trade policy. More concretely, measures restricting trade on environmental grounds should be allowable, even if not presently sanctioned by GATT/WTO; special trade promotion devices related to environmental objectives (such as export subsidies for pollution control equipment) should be allowed; trade restrictions to offset the effects of low environmental standards abroad should be allowed; and existing trade treaties (such as GATT/WTO, or the Treaty of Rome) should not preclude new environmental arrangements simply on grounds of precedent. According to this school of thought, what is needed is to develop appropriate global management strategies for scarce environmental resources; trade policies should be seen as one of several supporting mechanisms to implement such resource management.

The counter to this second line of argument is that any special treatment for the environment introduced into existing trade rules sets a dangerous precedent. This counterargument is put forward especially strongly by trade policy practitioners, who contend that a wide range of issues might follow the same path of linkage to trade as with the environment, with a "trade and . . ." label being used to justify special treatment. A domino theory of the trading system is sometimes raised, that is, special treatment for one issue will lead to special treatment for others, with, eventually, a disappearance of the rule regime in the trading system as we know it today. Related to and further elaborating this argument is the often-stated risk of environmental capture by protectionist interests using environmental arguments to legitimize their policy objectives.

Why has this debate come to the fore now, and why with such force? When environmental issues came four-square onto the economic policy agenda some 30 years ago, they were seen as highly localized, involving such matters as soil erosion, pesticide use, and congestion and air quality in urban areas, among others. Any international dimension was largely limited to identifiable cross-border effects, either within a region or bilaterally, such as those arising with acid rain.

However, since major environmental issues such as global warming and ozone depletion are now seen in the wider policy community as having worldwide implications, linkage between trade and environment in recent years has become a major policy issue. Such major environmental issues have become internationalized to an extraordinary degree, with clear global rather than regional environmental impact.[3] With this has come growing concern in some countries over domestic environmental practices, such as deforestation and management of the rain forests, in other countries. This has sparked debate on an apparent lack of environmental concern and action by the international institutions. The debate has focused on such bodies as the GATT and the WTO, the World Bank and the International Monetary Fund (IMF).

Fundamental to the debate is the question of "policy override," that is, whether some policy objectives are of such prime importance that they should dominate others. In the trade and environment debate, the override issue is whether environmental calamity is now sufficiently close that considerations of global environmental management dominate trade policy considerations.[4] The contention is that such considerations should outweigh the possibly adverse consequences for international trade of an increase in trade barriers aimed at achieving environmental goals. Moreover, if no other policy instruments beyond trade policy are available to achieve environmental policy objectives, then trade policy should be used for this purpose.

The environmental community argues that trade policy should no longer come first but, as noted above, should fit into a framework of sound global resource management policies, including management of environmental quality, as a supporting device.

. . . .
HOW SIGNIFICANT IS THE TRADE AND ENVIRONMENT CONFLICT?

■ THE POSITIONS TAKEN BY THE VARIOUS PROTAGONISTS can be couched in the form of two questions: How significant is the trade and environment conflict? What does the evidence suggest is the nature of the conflict?

As indicated above, the debate bifurcates. On the one hand, there is the extent of physical interdependence between trade and environment, that is, ways in which increased trade can itself be harmful for the environment through such measurable indicators as air and water quality; emissions of sulfur, carbon, and other harmful substances; increased risks of discharge of toxic wastes, and so on. On the other, there is the issue of policy conflict: whether or not trade policy should be used to achieve environmental objectives; who the gainers and losers are from such policies (whether environmental interests in rich countries, for instance, gain at the expense of low-income developing countries); and whether pre-existing trade treaties, such as GATT/WTO, unreasonably restrain the adoption of desirable environmental policy.

As to the first, there is much apparent evidence of a connection between environmental disrepair and trade-related activities. As noted above, the environmental destabilization in the maquiladora free trade zone in Mexico was directly attributed during the NAFTA debate to the growth of U.S.-Mexican trade. Without this trade, it was argued, the zone would not exist; and, in turn, these environmental ills would be absent. Deforestation and reduced forest cover coexisting alongside trade in tropical lumber were equally argued to demonstrate the link.

Of course, a causal link does not necessarily follow from simple observation of environmental damage alongside trade activity; the counterfactuals to be examined need to be carefully specified. In the case of the maquiladora zone, a number of alternative hypotheses that have not yet been clearly tested can be generated to explain the link. Thus, no one denies the data showing negative environmental effects in the zone, but equally, no one knows what the effect would be of a more limited trade regime.

There are several arguments that could be made against the view that more trade will worsen environmental quality in this case. First, the location in the maquiladora zone is induced by trade policies giving special treatment for imported inputs used in the zone. A withdrawal of these policies and reduced trade could see some industries relocate elsewhere in Mexico, thus spreading the environmental damage. Second, with reduced trade, the composition of production would change to increase production for the domestic market; the net impact of this on environmental quality is unclear. A third possible argument is that larger exports to a higher income country, such as the United States will tend to require those exports to meet foreign environmental standards if they are to sell in those markets. In this case, the argument would be that trade tends to raise environmental standards of products (though not necessarily the methods of production) toward those of the larger and higher income country.

For now these are merely counterarguments to the view that trade and environment are in conflict in such instances as maquiladora trade. But they have a ring of plausibility as would, probably, further counters to these counterhypotheses, creating a pattern of ambiguous effect to be found elsewhere in the trade and environment debate outside the maquiladora issues. Carlos Primo Braga, for instance, points out that log export bans in Indonesia have had the effect of encouraging on-shore plywood production in Indonesia;[5] but this uses old and inefficient cutting technology compared with off-shore (U.S.) production and, because of wastage, requires more logs per square foot of plywood. Thus, in case after case, the strength and direction of physical linkage between trade and environment are unclear.

The second prong of the debate between trade and environment emphasizes policy conflict and is more subtle. But here too, the nature and implications of links are ambiguous. Environmental advocates argue that it is reasonable to use trade policy as a penalty device to influence the environmental policies of countries unwilling to introduce changes to their domestic policy regimes that are needed from a global point of view. They also argue that it is reasonable for trade policy to be used to discourage artificial incentives in country policies that have adverse environmental consequences, such as the incentive for manufacturers to migrate to the lowest standard countries (so-called pollution havens).

They also see no difficulty with the idea that trade rules should be rewritten to allow for wide ranging environmental exceptions under existing rules in the GATT/WTO. This encompasses the override proposal whereby trade measures used with clear environmental intent should override any restrictions on them implied by existing international agreements, such as GATT/WTO. In new international trade negotiations, such as NAFTA, proponents of this measure usually also see it as appropriate to give trade provisions of environmental treaties precedence over existing trade treaties if they are in conflict. New trade rules giving latitude to importing countries to apply constraint of trade measures on environmental grounds thus lie at the heart of their advocacy.

In recent years, there have been several examples of conflict over these rules. A notable instance is the high profile GATT panel that in 1991 addressed the practices of tuna fishermen off the Mexican west coast. Tuna were being caught in nets that incidentally entangle dolphins, causing some of the dolphins to be killed. The United States made repeated representations to Mexico to reduce the number of dolphins killed in these tuna catches. Appealing to U.S. legislation under the Marine Mammal Protection Act, Earth Island Institute, a California nonprofit group, moved to ban the importation of canned, frozen, and fresh tuna into the United States from five countries (Ecuador, Mexico, Panama, Venezuela, and Vanuatu). The United States also had a labeling requirement under this law that canned tuna sold in the United States be labeled that the tuna was caught in a dolphin-friendly manner.

Mexico requested a GATT panel in this case, using two separate arguments. The first was that the United States had no rights under the GATT to impose such a trade ban. However, the United States asserted that under Article XX(b) of the GATT it had rights to use trade bans to protect endangered species. The Mexican counterargument was that there were no endangered species in this case; the only issue was the nature of the fishing methods used. The Mexicans also appealed the labeling requirement that canned tuna be displayed with a logo indicating that dolphin-friendly methods were used to catch the tuna. Their grounds were that this was a violation of the marks-of-origin provisions of the GATT under Article IV, which only requires an indication of country origin.

This request for a panel by Mexico, and the report which ruled in their favor, attracted widespread attention because it was the first time that a GATT panel was asked to rule on an environmental issue. Environmental groups made public representations in Geneva protesting the case and emphasizing their claim that the GATT was anti-environment. They maintained that concern for the dolphins, not profit, should have been the driving force behind the regulation of international trade in tuna.

In examining the pros and cons of such measures, trade economists have typically argued that trade policy is only second-best environmental policy; and that first-best policy would involve an explicit measure, such as a tax, for correcting an externality. If countries that are the source of environmental damage refuse to institute appropriate internalization of externalities, then it is accepted that trade actions may improve matters, but the effect could equally be to make things worse. Trade economists, therefore, tend to be cautious on the need for policy intervention in such cases. They are skeptical of such measures because of the risk of policy capture in which domestic groups use environmental arguments to legitimize the protection they seek from foreign competition.

The trade and environment policy dichotomy is especially sensitive for those in the trade policy community who, for several decades, have acted on the assumption that trade policy matters should be resolved solely on the basis of the traditional economic policy issues. Other issues, such as the environment, need not be considered in determining measures to improve the performance of the trading system. This perspective emerged from the global recession in the 1930s and the perceived linkage of trade to that recession, the subsequent rise of totalitarian regimes in Europe, and hence the military conflict of the 1940s. The GATT, nondiscrimination, and other key elements of the postwar trading system became viewed in the 1960s and 1970s as the bedrock of a structure whose central objective was to prevent any possibility of a return to the 1930s and subsequent continental war in Europe. Indeed, until the arrival of the trade and environment issue, the horrors of the 1930s and the 1940s and their links to trade were assumed to provide the rationale for defending the sanctity of global trade arrangements at all costs.

Before the Uruguay Round, successive attempts to place other policy objectives above trade also failed. In the early 1980s when the debt crisis hit the developing countries, special trade preferences were mooted in some circles to allow the heavily indebted countries to alleviate their debt by generating more foreign exchange from exports. But approaches to the GATT by the IMF arguing, along such lines, for trade preferences for heavily indebted countries, were rebuffed. The grounds were that the performance of the global economy was more important than reducing the severity of the debt problems of a subset of countries. Nondiscrimination remained the order of the day, with no trade preferences given to heavily indebted developing countries.

In the Uruguay Round, the separateness of the trading system as a policy subsystem was breached over the issue of intellectual property protection. This set the precedent for the arguments now heard in the trade and environment debate. Intellectual property protection was a low-profile issue until the period before the launch of the Round. After the launch the issue emerged as a key agenda item; intellectual property norms and standards were to be prescribed in the GATT, and, if necessary, enforced with trade sanctions. The resulting agreements set international standards for intellectual property production. The agreements allowed for dispute settlement to authorize cross-retaliation, if necessary involving trade measures on goods, for violation of intellectual property rights. In other words, trade measures were to be used to enforce non-trade arrangements.

Today, as a result, the environmental community can invoke these measures to press for similar measures to slow or reduce trade that has adverse environmental consequences. They ask for trade sanctions, where required, against countries whose domestic environmental policies threaten the environmental quality of others. They seek to use trade policy to offset incentives that promote environmentally damaging practices, such as incentive to locate environmentally harmful production in low standard countries; trade controls are sought to limit international flows of toxic waste. The policy component of the conflict between trade and environment thus clearly emerges as a central element in the debate.

During the Uruguay Round the trade and environment debate was also heightened by the argument made by the GATT Secretariat in 1992 that GATT Article XX exceptions permit import restrictions only if the environmental damage was generated by a product, not if it originated from the production process or method (PPM) that had been used to generate the product. This issue of PPMs (utilized by the Mexicans, as mentioned above, in the dolphin dispute) came to the fore again in the later stages of the Round.

Measures considered in these later discussions include those for environmental protection as well as regulations that apply to PPMs. The sanitary and phytosanitary measures and technical barriers to trade (TBT) agreements partially address problems raised by a number of contentious environmental cases, including the Canadian beer can case involving an environmental levy on beer packaged in cans.[6] The objective of these agreements is to minimize the extent to which standards and regulations have negative effects on trade, or act as disguised trade barriers, while still permitting GATT/WTO contracting parties to adopt or maintain standards that are necessary for the protection of human, plant, and animal life and health. Each agreement defines a national treatment obligation and a necessity test with the aim of minimizing adverse effects of measures taken, much as in GATT Article XX. Because the Uruguay Round disciplines in this area seemingly restrict domestic policies rather than border measures, they promise to be a source of ongoing conflict.

DEVELOPING COUNTRIES AND THE TRADE
AND ENVIRONMENT ISSUE

■ ENMESHED IN THE TRADE AND ENVIRONMENT DEBATE are the concerns of the developing countries, who see linkage of trade to environmental quality as being driven largely by environmental interests in the higher income countries.[7] Their implicit argument is that environmental quality is a luxury good and that the consumer preferences of the higher income countries are behind new proposed rules linking trade and environment. From their perspective these new rules largely involve threats of trade restrictions being placed on their exports to pressure them to change their environmental policies, while the richer industrialized countries seem not to be targeted. The outcome, they fear, will be truncated growth and development to satisfy conservation objectives set by outsiders. Developing countries, therefore, talk of developments in this area as reflecting "green imperialism" or "eco-imperialism," arguing that if the trading system continues to develop in this way, in the long run it can only be disadvantageous to their growth and development aspirations.

Tension is therefore growing between developed and developing countries on the issue of the linkage between trade and environment. On one side are the environmental advocates in industrial countries; on the other, are developing countries' own strong interest in pursuing trade-led developmental strategies free from environmental restrictions. In asserting their interests, the developing countries emphasize the extensive unilateral liberalization that has taken place in the developing world in the late 1980s and early 1990s. They point to the trade gains that have flowed from this and the strong support the approach has received from the industrial countries. Trade restrictions against developing countries in the name of environmental concerns of wealthy citizenry in the developed world seem to run counter to what developing countries have been encouraged to do in recent years within the trading system.

The implications of the trade and environment debate are seen by several developing countries in negative, and even hostile, terms. The issue for those countries is their ability to provide environmental quality at levels and in ways that will satisfy preferences in the developed world without jeopardizing growth in the developing world.

Developing countries base many of their arguments against linking trade policy to environmental policies on the primacy of national property rights. For instance, many in the South question the grounds on which the developed countries now assert rights over management of forests in developing countries and seek to restrain deforestation by developing countries, when developed countries' own deforestation was so clearly unrestrained.[8]

Developing countries are increasingly arguing that they should be compensated for environmental restraint, rather than subjected to trade-based retaliation against their environmental practices. As they see it, the rain forests are sovereign territory; if developed countries are concerned about forest cover they have the option of replanting trees in their own countries which they deforested decades and even centuries earlier. To the very vocal environmental groups in developed countries, the developing countries' forests represent the lungs of the earth, a communally owned resource to be managed on a global basis. Developing countries see a policy agenda emerging in the developed world that seeks to define the parameters of a global resource management regime, independently of their growth and development aspirations.

. . . .

IMPLICATIONS FOR PARTICIPATION IN THE TRADING SYSTEM AND THE WTO

■   ALL THE ABOVE ARGUMENTS AND DEVELOPMENTS have implications for the participation of developing countries in the trading system. In the 1960s, there was an escalation of North-South conflict over trade and its role in development. Developing countries were concerned with protecting infant industries and reducing endemic balance-of-payments deficits arising from poor export prospects. The view, then widely accepted, was that the trade problems of developing countries were fundamentally different from those of developed countries. This led in 1964 to the formation of UNCTAD, which was heavily influenced by the ideas of Raul Prebisch, and subsequently to a collective strategy pursued by the developing countries of seeking special and differential treatment in the trading system. Within the rules of the trading system, they sought both special rights to protect their own markets and preferential access to developed-country markets. Global political tensions on trade issues grew correspondingly as this position was advanced.

In recent decades this conflict has become ever more muted, as developing countries have, at best, seen only limited direct benefits from their protectionist strategies. The benefits of protection have been cast into further doubt by the rapid growth of outward-oriented economies in Asia. In the last ten years or so, many developing countries have unilaterally liberalized their trade policies, a virtual repudiation of their earlier call for special and differential treatment. Many developing countries also participated extensively in the Uruguay Round. The North-South conflict, as it evolved in the 1960s, seemed to recede during the Uruguay Round. As part of this process it became increasingly recognized that the countries of the South were themselves heterogeneous, with interests that often intersected with those of countries in the North, as well as with each other.

The trade and environment issue raises the probability that developing countries will resume a collective approach to trade issues, and that a North-South divide could reemerge on these issues. The potential for such a conflict is large. The cohesiveness of the interest in the developing world is established. The desire for compensation rather than retaliation is very strong. Moreover, the sense of being at a disadvantage to developed countries would be aggravated by the extensive use of measures to restrict trade on environmental grounds by developed countries.

The trade and environment issue also has implications for the fledgling WTO. In considering issues of intellectual property alongside those of trade, the Uruguay Round set a precedent for allowing trade measures to be linked with nontrade issues. Proposed uses of trade measures on environmental grounds and new trade rules to permit this represent a further extension of the precedent. This is sometimes characterized as the use of trade policy as a policeman, instead of as a policy measure in its own right.

A central issue is how far any precedent for using trade policy in this way should be allowed to spread, and to which other issues. After trade and environment, the concern is that trade and almost anything else could naturally follow. Indeed, this evolution in the system is clearly seen in the debate on trade and labor standards, which is discussed earlier in this volume by Rodrik. Thus, the trade and environmental debate poses a central question for the trading system and participants in any future negotiation: How far should the system be diluted with nontrade issues?

A series of more technical, system-related issues raised by the trade and environment debate remains to be resolved. This is because, until relatively recently, there had been few trade disputes, or even trade issues, of an environmental nature. Hence, even the interpretation of existing trade rules as they touched on environmental issues remained and still remains unclear. Two central questions were defined above in the discussion of the tuna/dolphin dispute between the United States and Mexico,[9] which raised issues under GATT/WTO Article XX. Article XX allows for general exceptions from GATT/WTO disciplines including, where individual products are concerned and under carefully specified conditions, environmental exceptions. Article III deals with the issues surrounding the use of trade measures because of concerns with production and processing methods used abroad, and the associated issues of national treatment. In the tuna/dolphin dispute, the United States claimed rights to protect on grounds of endangerment to dolphins, and Mexico claimed violation of their GATT/WTO rights since trade restrictions were used by the United States on the basis of how a product was produced, rather than the nature of the product itself.

Beyond the need to clarify the interpretation of existing trade rules, is the need for global institutions to coordinate and clarify the implied combined trade and environment rule regime they administer together. This need for joint action is especially necessary with respect to the emerging global environmental treaties.[10] In the case of ozone depletion, for instance, the Montreal Protocol contains trade provisions that, if used, will in all probability be in conflict with GATT/WTO. Which treaty has precedence over the other has not been resolved. Similar issues are likely to arise in future with any global agreement that seeks to limit carbon emissions.

As noted above, the trade policy community also worries significantly about the risk of policy capture in such circumstances. This danger has implications for the trading system because it compounds the central anxiety of trade policy practitioners that the trade and environment issue is the thin end of a wedge. They fear that it is only a part of a wider evolution of the trading system, through which the rule regime will be progressively weakened. They see green capture as something inherently difficult to prevent, once environmental exceptions are made, drawing parallels with the use of dumping procedures by protectionist interests in certain industries, when dumping by any meaningful economic definition seems unlikely to have occurred.

In summary, there are several implications for the trading system from these developments: first, a threatened fragmentation of the trading system from the introduction of nontrade issues into trade negotiation; second, a need to clarify the application of existing trade rules to environmental issues; and, third, the evolving institutional linkage between the WTO, other global institutions, and emerging global treaties in the environmental area. For now, these remain separate stand-alone treaties, but they may eventually be consolidated under a wider institutional heading, posing a further challenge to current trade institutions.

. . . .

WHAT TO DO?

■ THIS DISCUSSION RAISES OBVIOUS QUESTIONS about how to proceed on the trade and environment issue, especially for developing countries. Is there a clear position they should adopt on whether trade rules should be rewritten? What seems the most likely outcome, and with what implications for the developing countries? How serious is the trade and environment issue for the developing countries? Is there potential for a common developing-country position on this issue?

On the specifics of the possible ways forward on the trade rules front, there are conflicting views as to what can and should be done from a global interest point of view, and what the developing countries should do. There have been suggestions made, for instance, of introducing a new general exception under GATT/WTO allowing use of trade measures where used for environmental intent, as a way of dealing with trade and environmental linkage. But the obvious difficulty here is that a loosely worded exception allows for wide ranging departures from existing GATT/WTO disciplines, while a tightly worded and constrained exception is both hard to draft and difficult to enforce. Another suggestion that has been made is to encourage the use of GATT/WTO waivers to deal with trade and environment problems; but waivers require unanimity in the GATT/WTO, and in other areas (such as agriculture) the idea at present is to phase them out, not to introduce new ones. Again, no consensus exists on whether to proceed in this way.

Another suggestion that has been made is to negotiate environmental revisions to present GATT/WTO articles, perhaps in a special trade and environment miniround. Many problems arise here, not the least of which is that nearly every GATT/WTO article could potentially be argued to be subject to rewriting on environmental grounds. This could include export subsidies (Article XVI) where subsidies to exports of pollution control equipment might be argued allowable; Article XIX where environmental concerns in safeguards actions might merit special treatment; and Article XXIV where environmental impact analyses of regional trade agreements might be required, on and on through all the GATT/WTO articles. Even basic GATT/WTO principles, such as most favored nation (MFN), might be argued as breachable on environmental grounds since countries might wish to claim rights under Article I to target particular countries that are the source of environmental problems. Again there is no consensus either on the feasibility or the desirability of entering into such a negotiation.

Finally, more targeted approaches to the trade and environment issue have been proposed, such as revising GATT/WTO Article XX to clarify its environmental content. Even here there is debate. Clarification of GATT/WTO articles has proceeded in the past via the dispute settlement/panel report route, which therefore might seem the obvious approach to Article XX. However, existing panel reports in this area, including the tuna/dolphin draft report, have been attacked from some quarters as unsound, raising issues as to the reliability of the panel process in this area.

For the developing countries, the specifics of a trade and environment negotiation in GATT/WTO remain somewhat vague. There are mixed opinions as to the merits of alternative approaches: The interests of the developing countries have also not been extensively debated. Their instinct seems to be that the trade and environment issue threatens to impose on them new trade barriers in the name of environmental protection, and this runs counter to their rights to use the trading system to achieve their growth and development.

This leaves the question as to how the developing countries might or should respond to the trade and environment debate, and a few key points emerge from the discussion above. Perhaps the most important is that at all levels the debate remains inconclusive, and hence policy responses are as yet poorly framed. The evidence marshalled by environmental groups as to how trade and environment interact has been challenged, and strongly so in some quarters. Every proposal offered as to how to proceed to change trade rules has encountered opposition and difficulty. There is no consensus on what needs to be done, how to do it, or the impacts that would follow.

Thus, time is on the side of the developing countries as they contemplate how to respond. The GATT/WTO working party on trade and environment set up at the Marakesh meeting that concluded the Round is to report at the ministerial meeting in Singapore in 1996, but it only has a brief to explore and elaborate on what trade and environment linkages are. No proposals for change are to be offered. Beyond this, several years will be required to develop a negotiating agenda, and even more time will be needed for its successful conclusion. And, unless trade and environment were part of a wider agenda, the potential for negotiating progress on trade and environment issues through exchanges of concessions would almost certainly be limited. Put simply, developing countries will almost certainly have a fair amount of time to frame their response and participate in this process.

However, while time may be available it is still finite, and there is a need to clearly delineate the developing-country interest in this area. It is also important to recognize that their interests are far from homogeneous either across countries or across topics. Thus, rights to protect on environmental grounds might be resisted by developing countries as potentially truncating their growth and development, but such rights have also been sought by developing countries as a way of controlling imports of toxic waste for treatment by disreputable companies. Controls on imports of tropical lumber would be resisted by Brazil, Southeast Asian countries, and others with tropical forests but might benefit transition economies, such as Russia, that have temperate zone lumber to export.

Thus, one problem in developing a negotiating position will be to explore how strong the common interest is, and in which issues. Are calls for compensation universally shared, and who should receive what? Are all environment-related uses of trade policy to be resisted, or are some (such as in toxic waste) to be accepted? Which environment-related uses of trade policy could conceivably be traded away for relaxation in other policy areas (such as, say, immigration controls)?

The trade and environment debate, at least as far as the developing countries are involved, may well disintegrate into conflict and discord. Disagreements encompass conflict over countries' rights to use their environmental resources for development versus the claimed rights of others to limit their use of these resources on global environmental quality grounds; conflict over rights to use environmental resources to achieve development now due to the developing countries on the grounds they should not be asked that present day global environmental problems reflect the earlier and current misuse of such resources by developed countries; and conflict over the communal rights asserted by developed countries to protect remaining resources as being in the global interest. Within this ambiguity also lurks the threat of trade policy being used to police rather than to achieve improved performance from the trading system. And along with this are the dangers of policy capture and environmental legitimization by protectionist interests.

Developing countries have been profoundly disturbed by the way the trade and environment debate has evolved thus far within the trading system. But environmental groups are also disturbed by the developing-country reaction to their concerns. This is particularly true because their commitment to sustainable development usually goes hand-in-hand with concerns about global poverty that ally them with developing countries on other issues. How all these concerns interact and develop will, in part, shape any future negotiation on this issue, and the developing-country interest in it will play a central role. As of now, developing countries have time to more clearly develop and articulate their interests and arguments; and at the end of the day the need to alleviate poverty may prove as powerful a political force in this debate as the risk of further environmental degradation.

Notes

This paper benefited from comments from Christine Contee, Catherine Gwin, Robert Lawrence, Carlos Primo Braga, Dani Rodrik, Sidney Weintraub, and participants at an ODC workshop held in Washington, DC, May 1995.

[1] See the discussions of this issue in K. Anderson and R. Blackhurst, eds., *The Greening of World Trade Issues* (Hartfordshire, UK: Harvester Wheatsheaf for the GATT, 1993); C. Nelder-Corvari, *The Greening of GATT: Trade and the Environment*, Department of Finance Working Paper (Ottawa: Government of Canada, 1989); and P. Uimonen and J. Whalley, *The Trade and Environment Issue After the Uruguay Round* (New York: Macmillan, forthcoming).

[2] Leonard and Christensen provide an eloquent statement of these types of arguments in the context of U.S.-Mexico trade and specifically the environmental considerations in the NAFTA debate. See R. Leonard and E. Christensen, "Testimony on Behalf of the Community Nutrition Institute Before the International Trade Commission Hearing on Economic Effects of a Free Trade Agreement Between Mexico and the United States," 12 April 1991.

[3] See D. Pearce et al., "World Economy, World Environment," *The World Economy*, Vol. 15 (1992), pp. 295–313.

[4] For an early discussion of these arguments as the trade and environment issue was unfolding, see J. Whalley, "The Interface Between Environmental and Trade Policies," *Economic Journal*, Vol. 101, No. 405 (1991), pp. 180–89.

[5] Carlos Primo Braga, "Tropical Forests and Trade Policy: The Case of Indonesia and Brazil," in *International Trade and the Environment*, ed. P. Low, World Bank Discussion Paper No. 159 (Washington, DC: World Bank, 1992).

[6] In its annual budget on April 30, 1992, the province of Ontario introduced an "environmental levy" of 10 cents per can of beer. The tax did not apply to soft drink cans. As most U.S. beer exported to Canada is in cans, the United States believed the tax was for protectionist purposes.

[7] See the more extensive discussion of the developing-country position on these issues in J. Whalley, "Competition or Retaliation: Developed and Developing Countries and the Growing Conflict Over Global Environmental Conservation," Working Paper (Washington, DC: Institute for Policy Reform, May 1994).

[8] For analysis of the environmental implications of trade in forestry products, see E. Barbier, B. Aylward, J. Burgess, and J. Bishop, "Environmental Effects of Trade in the Forestry Sector" (London: International Institute for Environment and Development, 1991, mimeo).

[9] See *International Trade Reporter*, "U.S. District Court Orders Ban on Imports of Certain Tuna Because of Dolphin Kills" (12 October 1990) and "Appeals Panel Hears Merits of Embargo on Mexican Tuna Based on Dolphin Kills" (20 February 1991).

[10] For some thoughts on how to address some of these conflicts, see E. U. Petersmann, "International Trade Law and International Environmental Law: Prevention and Settlement of International Environmental Disputes in GATT," *Journal of World Trade*, Vol. 27, No. 1, pp. 43–81.

About the Authors

ROBERT Z. LAWRENCE is the Albert L. Williams Professor of International Trade and Investment at the Kennedy School of Government, Harvard University. He is also a non-resident Senior Fellow at the Brookings Institution, a Research Associate of the National Bureau of Economic Research, a Program Associate of the Overseas Development Council, and Chair of the Project on Middle East Trade at Harvard's Institute for Social and Economic Policy in the Middle East. His books on international economics include *Regionalism, Multilateralism and Deeper Integration* (Brookings Institution, 1996); *Single World, Divided Nations: The Impact of Trade on OECD Labor Markets* (Brookings Institution and the OECD Development Centre, 1996); and with Albert Bressand and Takatoshi Ito, *A Vision for the World Economy* (Brookings Institution, 1996).

DANI RODRIK is the Rafiq Hariri Professor of International Political Economy at the John F. Kennedy School of Government, Harvard University, and a Program Associate of the Overseas Development Council. Before joining the Harvard faculty, he was Professor of Economic and International Affairs at Columbia University. He is also a Research Associate of the National Bureau of Economic Research and Research Fellow of the Centre for Economic Policy Research. He is author of *Eastern Europe and the Soviet Union in the World Economy* (Institute for International Economics, 1991); co-editor of *The Economics of Middle East Peace* (MIT Press, 1993); co-author of *Miracle or Design? Lessons from the East Asian Experience* (ODC, 1994); and author of many articles on trade policy, economic development, and political economy in professional journals.

JOHN WHALLEY is Professor of Economics at the University of Western Ontario, London, Canada, and Professor of Development and International Economics at the University of Warwick (UK). He is also a Research Associate of the National Bureau of Economic Research, a Fellow of the Econometric Society, and a Fellow of the Royal Society of Canada. He has written widely on trade and development issues and co-edits the journal, *The World Economy*.

About the ODC

ODC is an international policy research institute based in Washington, D.C. that seeks to inform and improve the multilateral approaches and institutions—both global and regional—that play increasingly important roles in the promotion of development and the management of related global problems.

ODC's program of multilateral analysis and dialogue is designed to explore ideas and approaches for enhancing global cooperation, to build networks of new leadership among public and private actors around the world, and to inform decision making on selected development topics of broad international concern.

ODC is a private, nonprofit organization funded by foundations, corporations, governments, and private individuals.

Stephen J. Friedman is the Chairman of the Overseas Development Council, and the Council's President is John W. Sewell.

ODC
1875 Connecticut Avenue, NW
Suite 1012
Washington, DC 20009
(202) 234-8701

ODC Board of Directors

Also in ODC's Policy Essay Series:

Moving to the Market: The World Bank in Transition

Richard W. Richardson and Jonas H. Haralz

The development paradigm is shifting, and the private sector now holds center stage as the lead player in economic development. In recent years the World Bank has been pressed by its member governments to rethink its role in private sector development. This Policy Essay reviews the initiatives taken by the World Bank and the International Finance Corporation and makes recommendations for the future.

"a thought-provoking and very relevant contribution"
 —*Michael Bruno*
  Vice President of Development Economics and Chief Economist, The World Bank

Policy Essay No. 17, 1995, 108 pp.
ISBN: 1-56517-023-7   *$13.95*

Poverty and Inequality in Latin America: Past Evidence, Future Prospects

Samuel A. Morley

For all the countries of Latin America, the 1980s was a period of unprecedented adjustment. Most countries faithfully applied the orthodox medicine of real devaluation and fiscal deficit reduction. In every country there was a contradictory recession. The costs of this adjustment were high. For the region as a whole, per capita income fell by 11 percent over the decade. The lengthy and almost universal decline in living standards was unprecedented in Latin America. In this Policy Essay, Samuel Morley describes what happened to the distribution of income and to poverty during the painful decade and offers some long-run prospects for the region based on what has happened since 1990. The author also draws some tentative conclusions on the relationship between poverty and distribution on the one hand and macroeconomic conditions and economic structure on the other.

Policy Essay No. 13, 1994, 100 pp.
ISBN: 1-56517-020-2   *$13.95*

Miracle or Design? Lessons from the East Asian Experience

Albert Fishlow, Catherine Gwin, Stephan Haggard, Dani Rodrik, and Robert Wade

There is little debate that the developing countries of East and Southeast Asia have been highly successful in achieving rapid, export-led growth. How they accomplished this feat is much more controversial. The World Bank's 1993 study, The East Asian Miracle, offers an interpretation that focuses heavily on the success of market-oriented reform. This Policy Essay summarizes what the World Bank says about the East Asian experience and presents three critical essays in which the authors draw conclusions on the report, and on the economic lessons for other developing countries in the East Asian experience.

Policy Essay No. 11, 1994, 128 pp.
ISBN: 1-56517-015-6   *$13.95*

To order, call Johns Hopkins University Press at 1-800-537-5487 (inside U.S.) or 1-410-516-6957 (outside U.S.). Or write:

Johns Hopkins University Press
2715 N. Charles Street
Baltimore, MD 21218-4319